'JUST MY NOTES'

Navigating your way through life's oddities

Shelley James

British Library Cataloguing in Publication Data.
A catalogue record for this book is available from the British Library

ISBN 978 0 86071 775 1

A Commissioned Publication Printed by

MOORLEYS
Print, Design & Publishing
email: info@moorleys.co.uk · website: www.moorleys.co.uk

From the author of 'Carry Me Back To The 70's' comes 'Just My Notes'. Anecdotes covering five decades of how life can sometimes present you with the strangest and funniest of predicaments when you least expect them.

"I've always enjoyed the process of writing letters to my friends, and I hope that comes across in this book. It's 'just me', chatting to 'just you'.

Introduction.

*Should anyone ask me why I constantly write things down in diaries, note pads etc, then I'd have to be honest and say "I haven't a clue really", it's just something that I've done since being a child. I remember getting my first diary. It was a Christmas present and I was six! It had a pretty picture on the front of a little girl picking petals from a daisy, and I can hear my Dad now saying to my Mum as I opened it and proudly presented it to her...
"What's the point in that for a 6 year owd? It's like giving a bald chap a comb".
But how wrong he was.....
The book cover was very attractive so regardless of what its life destiny was, I loved it.
Later that day on re-visiting and looking at the Christmas gifts in detail with Mum, she explained to me what a diary was and how they were used.....and so it began.*

Monday..........."Went shooping with Mum"
Tuesday..........."Beverly come to play"
Wednesday......."Dogs been sick"

*Hey, don't knock it, If only life was that straight forward now. The scribbles would happen each day, or there would be a mass scribble of highlights at the end of each week. And did you notice shooping with Mum? Obviously it was shopping, but I copied exactly as I found it in that first diary, and hey, shooping always worked for Cher!
What I do find strange is you can go years thinking 'oh, nothing ever changes'. However, go back into your diary and you'll see sure enough there are changes happening*

all the time. It's just a little more subtle than the obvious life circle we all encounter of hatched, matched and dispatched.

So here's the thing, not wanting to send you, my reader, into a pit of misery these note book/diary memories are of the more light hearted nature.

Whilst on investigation I came across quite a few sad times and woes, (*channels the pop band 'Human League' and sings 'I'm only human'*) I feel however no-one wants to read about overdrafts, four hour traffic jams and family fall outs, not even me. So choosing carefully through the years of memories, these tales of the unexpected are all in some obscure way linked with the business of 'show'. Whether it be full-on stage shenanigans or that old 'being in that place at that time' then this probably wouldn't have happened to me.

Will this book give you all the answers to the meaning of life? I doubt that very much. Will it be 'life changing' perhaps? Nah! Not so much. But if it makes you smile, possibly relate to something once.......I feel, my work here is done.

We all have these bizarre often comical experiences in our lives, I'm sure of that. The only difference is I wrote mine down. I hope you enjoy the selection I've plucked from the pages of time. If nothing else it will make your own life appear moderately sane!

Dedicated to 'Mum'.

Caregiver, confidant, hug provider,
protector, advisor, and the best friend any girl
could have had. xxx

Contents

Chapter One... I Saw Her Standing There

In the 1960's and early 70's as a child, if you sat watching the T.V. a little later than usual, maybe school holidays or at the weekends, then if something came onto the TV that the programme makers thought wasn't really suitable for children's viewing, or folk of a nervous disposition, then they would put a small triangle in the corner of the screen, just as a little 'unsuitable for' warning. To be honest that just made it all the more enticing, and even though I would have been told "no, upstairs now, you can't watch this", it became a mission to get a sneaky peek! Although we didn't have colour television at the time I always saw it as a red triangle. As the years went on I found that quite profound. Why would I have imagined that triangle to be red? I was just a nipper, the seriousness of danger hadn't even registered at that age. Could it have possibly been society planting seeds in a subliminal way I wonder? Perhaps that idea of a warning sign should've been extended to real life. For example you're passing by a shop.........a bakery perhaps? and you're dieting............maybe that extra nudge would be helpful. *Man holds triangle outside shop* Calorie alert, calorie alert! We did go through a phase on TV of the triangle becoming extinct and practically everything being up for grabs, no triangle and no warnings, recently however we seem to have gone from one extreme to the other with a warning, it seems, before every TV show there is a warning of some sort. Does this happen before cartoons? I know the Tom and Jerry cartoons were labeled as 'violent' not so many years ago by the 'suck all the fun out of everything squad'. Let's not be hasty, they had a point, many a time I've seen people being chased around in a circle only to be bopped on the head by someone holding a frying pan and hearing a 'boiiiing' sound......what?

The expertise of the make-up artists and special effects on T.V. and film has certainly moved on since the days of Pinky and Perky.

I dread to think what my Nana would make of some of the TV screened nowadays. The BBC1 programme's 'Casualty' and 'Call the Midwife' for example are very graphic and realistic. I can hear her now, "Ow I say, tut tut tut". I mean, she used to get miffed if Harry Secombe did 'Highway' without a tie on.

Well I hope your sitting comfortably as we now delve into, 'Memories of a Grandmother' (even though she really didn't like the term Grandmother, in fact she hated it, hence Nana).

TV detector vans........If she noticed one out of her window patrolling the streets, she would turn her television off. Why? Well not what you're thinking, she had a licence, however her reasoning was,
"What happens if they knock at my door and I can't find my licence in time"!
Not sure what she expected them to do to her, 40 lashes with a whip in the market square maybe?

Budgies........She had a little yellow budgie, and while she was away on holiday, and it was in our care, it sadly died. That is what's known as 'sods law', as not only were we A1 with animals my Dad also had his own aviary with a variety of birds in, so she knew the budgie would be in good hands. 'Dusty' passed away 3 days after being in our care, it was awful. We came downstairs and he just lay on the bottom of his cage. Why? Why when he was in our care did this happen, my Mum and I sensibly going into panic central, while my Dad walked up to the cage and said,

"Oh dear, ya timing's a bit off Dusty. Gerra box our Blue, we'll bury him then I'll go an' ave a word with Tom up at Woodhouse" (Tom being a breeder of budgies/parakeets etc). Not wanting Nana to come back home to that sort of news at the end of her holiday, later that afternoon after Mum had fettled the cage Dad returned with a beautiful yellow budgie, an identical yellow boy.

"Owwww you can't tell at all Tony" Mum announced on giving the bird the once over.

"It just looks like he's had a good holiday" She said. And my Dad rolled his eyes.

On the day of Nana's return, ohhhh the stress as we all sat watching her holding our breath as she walked up to the cage blowing kisses and saying,

"'ello Dusty, 'ello then, have you been a good boy". While Dusty II did a very good impression of his predecessor, and whistled a merry tune to his heart's content, he didn't fully read the script, so while Nana never suspected anything, all she said a few weeks later was,

"It's funny isn't it, Dusty hasn't made that noise like a ping-pong ball bouncing (he really did), and chunter to me all day like he normally does ever since I've been back, no, nothing. He must be sulking 'cos I didn't take him on holiday"........

Yes, 'cos budgies do hold grudges don't they.

The alias Dusty passed away 3 years later and as Nana explained to her friends,

"He did everso well bless him, he was 6 ya know".........ummm.

Phones........I never saw her answer a phone. Her excuse was very straight forward.

"What if it's a man"!

So I 'spose my question is, 'how much exactly should we be protected from'? Surely there is a line between common sense and just ridiculous. You can't protect everyone from everything. Unless you move to a desert island, although I'm sure moving to one would bring up a whole host of other dangers and problems.

As I was growing up my Mum and Dad worked at a venue called 'The Piccadilly Club'. It was a great place actually. Along with local acts etc they would often have on well known entertainers too. I remember my Dad going ga-ga about Bert Weedon the infamous guitarist performing there one Saturday night.
"Ow eh, he can make that guitar talk" he praised.
I loved going in with Mum because if the resident musicians were there I was allowed to sing on the microphone and they would back me......in 'the' big room! The show room....actually 'on' the stage.....not the small bar! Best job my Mum ever had from my point of view.
Jean, the manager, was this very classy lady, always looked immaculate and stylish. She was very kind to me, even though I was younger than her own children I had the same privileges they did, so I could go in and see shows, just so long as I behaved, as if I would do anything other than that!
It was my first taste of singing with a live band, so from age 7 – 12 I felt very fortunate and spoilt. Miles the keyboard player in the band would always call me up onto the stage when they were doing a sound check.
"We need to get you up one night so that the customers can hear you" he said "I'll have a word with Jean". I stood open mouthed thinking, 'crikey, this was like, well, singing in a real world'!
Fingers crossed she would agree to it, and also that she wouldn't allow it. I really wanted to, but was nervous all at the same time.
A little later on Jean came out of her office and Miles called her

over, they stood chatting and laughing and then they both turned and looked at me.

"Would you like to get up and do a song in a few weeks then"? Miles called.

"Ow yes please" I called back standing crossed legged and fidgeting with my dress hem.

"Is that alright with you Mum"? said Jean calling over to my Mum.

"Yes, of course it is, as long as it's alright with you Jean. She'd love that wouldn't you duckie" said Mum smiling at me.

Jean carried on "right then, we'll have to see if we can get you a nice sparkly top to wear".

Owwwwww, I mean, owwwwwwwwww.

This was, without a single doubt my biggest thrill since the free gift fairy charm bracelet in 'Bunty' magazine. Well that and getting a goldfish for two saucepans from the rag and bone man. Growing up in the 60's ya see.........never mind those who were indulging in sex, drugs, rock and roll at the time..........it was all Bunty, Goldfish and Jelly Babies as far as I was concerned.

I recall The Who had a record out called 'I Can See for Miles'. This, for some strange 'kid-like' reason cracked me up. I sang it to Miles one day and couldn't get through it for laughing. My Mum looked on saying "She was like this at home Miles practicing it to sing to you, she's crackers".

I never did finish that song. Just trying to get through the first few lines each time I saw him would have me in raptures.

"I can see for miles tee hee and miles tee hee........" It just really amused me!

Mum and Dad didn't always work at the club at the same time, so there was one Sunday morning I went in with my Dad.

"Go and sit in there ma duck" said my Dad gesturing towards the small bar area, "Jukebox bloke'll be 'ere in a bit"

'The Jukebox man' (obviously his real name............or it should have been) had seen my Dad two weeks previously and told him "I'm back in a couple of weeks, bring ya little 'un in and she can have some records". Yep, I loved 'The Jukebox Man'. He was responsible for keeping all the 'tunes' up to date in the jukebox with the ever changing pop charts. After sitting in the club for an hour fussing the clubs guard dog 'Flash' and chatting to the cleaners (...talk to anyone me), in walked the jukebox man. It was so exciting. He opened up the jukebox, and took out lots of singles, then replaced them with shiny new records. He'd then let me choose 2 or 3 to play while he went to the office to do all the paper work. One of the first records he gave me was 'Boom Oo Yata-Ta-Ta' by Morecambe and Wise. He kept promising it to me but it was so popular on the jukebox he couldn't remove it. When the time came to replace it I wasn't at the club so he left it with one of the staff members for me. I still have it, it's practically an antique.

"Right then" he said looking at me "do you think you could make use of these" and passed me approximately 20 records.

"Ooowww thankyou" I said looking at the freebie goodies.

"Ya might not want 'em all so give away the ones you don't want eh good girl". And off he went but not before leaving me with half a dozen plastic record centres.

I had quite a romance with this place, Jean (also known to me as Auntie Jean) was such a lovely lady, I was allowed to stay in her flat above the club and play when the parents had extra long work days, I got to sing with the band and I was given free records, and..........sshhh don't tell anyone, but when the chap called to empty the one arm bandits he would always throw some odd coins in my direction………..arrrhhh………this place ticked all the boxes, even before it was the trend to say that!

Around 40 minutes after 'The Jukebox Man' left, my Dad walked by "ya alright Blue, what ya got there"? And I told him the title of each and every record I'd just been given, regardless if he was listening or not!

It was approaching midday at this point. "Right ma duck" he carried on, taking away my now empty bottle of Dandelion and Burdock. "let's geroff home". We walked towards the main doors and he stopped "Ow a-up I've forgot the keys, I'll need them for tomorrow" he said. "You wait in here, don't go out of here will ya" he said opening the door to 'Auntie Jeans' office and then closing it behind him. He tapped on the glass and mouthed, "I'll be 2 minutes". Never is, is it. When anyone says I'll be two minutes, what they actually mean is, 'I could be anything up to a quarter of an hour, possibly half an hour, but that would sound like a lot of hanging about, so I'll shorten it to two minutes in the hope I can dupe you into believing me'. And as I thought I had been conned. I sat in Auntie's office on her swivel chair spinning around and around, and after 10 minutes of the 2 minutes! I got a little bored.

"Dad" I called…………………."Dad"………………………..still spinning …………."DAD"……….."DAAAAAAAD", But nothing.

He'd told me not to go out of the office, but surely that meant don't go out of the building, after all I'd been 'in' the building all morning practically. So I wandered over to the door and on opening it I leaned in the doorway. Almost like being at a fairground I could hear things coming at me from all directions. I could hear music from the jukebox seeping out from the small bar and I could hear the bouncers chatting to each other at the doors to the right of me and around the corner in the main room I could hear music.

"Dad" I called again..........................."Daaaaaaad".

But again, no Dad.

I decided he would 'want' me to find him at this point......so that 'I' didn't worry! Well, I'd convinced myself that was what he'd want. Picking up my records I made my way to the double doors that led into the main room, they were closed. The bottom half of the door was wood and the top half frosted glass so I couldn't see in but I could hear customers cheering from inside.

"Oww I wonder what's happening in there" I thought as I took a few little steps closer. I prized open the doors by a few inches and on tip-toe peeped through. It had a mixed aroma of beer, smoke and aftershave. I couldn't quite see in the room as a few men were standing up at the back, but the music ended and they sat down. A compare came onto the stage and introduced a lady who swept onto the stage in a very glamorous sparkly outfit.

'Owww sparkles' I thought...........'I'll just wait here a while and watch the pretty lady, I'm sure my Dad won't be long now'.

The music was loud and the lady paraded up and down the stage in her long silver sequin dress, it had a split up on one side and every now and again she would show her leg, much to the amusement it seemed of the audience. She twirled and swirled on the stage and the audience cheered her on. A couple of minutes into the music and she took her gloves off.

"Oww she must be warm" I thought. She carried on dancing.

A few moments later she unzipped the back of her dress whilst facing the back of the stage.

Again I was thinking "Oww she must be 'really' warm".

The crowd we're getting louder and the sparkly dress was now heading south.........as in slipping 'off' the lady and onto the floor.

"Oh, that's strange" I thought "I wonder why she didn't go to the dressing room to do that". Could it be I was watching a quick change artiste?

I was 8 years old!

She was left wearing a silver sequin bikini and with her black feather boa draped over her shoulder, again she paraded up and down the stage and wiggled her way in front of the by now, engaged but noisy audience. They clapped and cheered and began shouting.

The lady then swooshed the feather boa over her head several times and then threw it into the audience and began to undo her bikini top…………………………eh!?

…………and then most surprisingly, and shockingly……………she took the bikini top off!!!!! She swung it around a while before she flung it to the back of the stage…………………………………Ow!!!!!

Oh dear………….this didn't feel right. Did she mean to do that? Should I be watching this? So in a mad panic I did a quick about turn and went 'thud' straight into my Dad who had just come down the stairs at the side of the doors. He didn't look happy.

"I said DON'T come out of the office, what are you doing 'ere"? He barked at me.

But I was mortified, I couldn't speak.

"I……………I……………I" was my reply, in a crude imitation of Carmen Miranda!

"What have you been doing? You didn't go into the show bar did ya, DID YA"? He asked angrily.

"Erm, I just had a little peep to see where you were". I said all shaky.

"Well, I wasn't in there was I" He said, and I was escorted out of the main doors by my elbow, feet hardly touching the floor and towards the car park. He seemed annoyed yet awkward.

"I TOLD you NOT to go out of Auntie Jeans office, you should've done as you we're told".

And he was right. I shouldn't have left the office….my poor eyes.

Getting into the car I held onto my latest record collection and we traveled home in silence, neither of us uttering a word. While it was still done in silence my Dad acknowledged a fellow traveler who had the same make car as himself, nice that, I absolutely loved that as a child. We didn't know these people and yet because we had a Reliant, other Reliant drivers would pap their horns or wave, and come on, who remembers the RAC man saluting!? Is it rose coloured glasses or were things actually classier back then? In my childhood years I had nothing to compare it to, but looking back........men wore ties.......and women didn't go to the shop in their pajamas!

When we reached home which was a relatively short journey of around 6 or 7 minutes, I went straight upstairs to play my records.

After about half an hour Mum came into my bedroom. She perched herself on the edge of my bed.

"............Are you alright duckie" she asked.

"Umm yes, I think so" I said.

"I see you've been given some records then, did you have a nice time at the club"? She enquired.

"Umm Yes, I th-i-nk so" I replied, this time looking down at the records.

"Your Dad's just been telling me you saw a lady dancing at the club today. Is that right"?

Questions.......questions, why so many questions.

I became very hot, 'Oh no, I'm going to get told off by my Mum as well' I thought.

I decided to test the water first.

"If I say yes, will I get into trouble"? I innocently asked.

My Mum looked down at me and smiled. "Well, if it's the truth, no, no you won't get into trouble".

'I'd better own up' I thought. "Yes, I did see a lady dancing, but it was only because my Dad was a long time and I didn't know where he'd gone and she had a sparkly dress on and the music was playing and he said he was going to be two minutes and he wasn't and, and, and.........."

Mum interrupted "alright, alright, steady.....so, did you see anything that praps' you thought you shouldn't have"?

I felt so embarrassed that I 'had', and I don't know why, but I just said "I don't t-h-i-n-k so".

"Alright then" said Mum "I'm going downstairs now to make some tea, but if you want to talk to me about anything you can".

After playing my records I eventually went downstairs.

The TV was on and my Dad was fixated in looking directly at the television. He didn't look at me at all.

'Oh he must be really annoyed with me' I thought.

Eventually the day rolled on and bedtime arrived. The following day Auntie Jean's eldest son had popped over on his pushbike with a small package, for me!

"Ow what have you got there" asked Mum.

"It's a present from Auntie Jean" I said.

I opened up the boutique bag to find a pretty sparkly pink top.

"Oww duckie that's lovely, you must say thank you next time you see Auntie Jean". I didn't have long to wait, four days later I was at the club with my Mum and Jean walked in looking like a film star with her blonde hair and red lips.

"Hello sweetheart" she said "do you like your little blouse".

"I love it, thank you" I said.

"That's good, because we'd like you to sing at the weekend, you could wear it then" she suggested.

Sing? At the weekend? Me? On stage? Me? Uh...........all these thoughts going around my head, I felt sick.

Now, maybe I had/have an over active imagination.........but I was horrified. There was no way they were going to get me onto that stage.

I'd seen what happened to people that wore sparkly tops, and I didn't want to be the next victim.

After a couple of hours Mum had finished and we walked home. I was so choked I couldn't speak, and what excuse exactly was I to come up with in order NOT to sing at the weekend.

"You're very quiet" Mum stated. "Is everything alright? "I thought you'd be excited about the weekend".

"Yes" I said like a little mouse.

"Are you sure? You don't appear to be" said Mum.

"Yes" I squeaked again, this time feeling hot and bothered.

"Ow duckie are you sure? It's not like you this. You're very quiet. You would tell me if something was wrong wouldn't you"? she said. And just as our house became in sight down the long road I just burst into tears.

"Oh dear, whatever is the matter" said my worried Mum.

"I don't, I don't, I don't want to..." I blubbered.

"You don't want to what"? She asked. Poor Mum, she looked very worried.

"I don't want to take my clothes off" I cried.

"YOU DON'T WANT TO TAKE YOUR CLOTHES OFF, eh? Why would you say that, what do you mean" asked my concerned if not confused Mum.

"I don't want to take my clothes off because that's what you have to do when you've got a sparkly top on"...........and the tale of my peeping Tom expose was out there in full.

There was a silence that came with the most reassuring Mum type hug and then she said,

"Oh duckie, you don't have to". She hugged me, consoled me and reassured me some more.

"Listen to me, that lady you saw, she's……er…….she's a special dancer, a very special dancer. You don't have to take any clothes off on stage, ever, PLEASE don't worry".

During the latter part of our walk home we talked it all out. I asked lots of questions and with clear information coming back from Mum easing my worried little head, I felt much happier.

On arriving home my Mum summoned my Dad to the kitchen where I believe judging by the tone of Mums voice he was being well and truly told off!

My Dad was very embarrassed, hence why he hadn't explained anything to me the day I saw the 'special dancer', and also why he hadn't been able to give me eye contact once we were home.

I sat at the bottom of the stairs and as my Dad came out of the kitchen followed by Trixie our dog, he looked at me and half whispered "You've just got me into trouble you have"……….he then shook his head and said 'shall we take Trixie for a walk to the shop and get some chocolate"………..Huh, as if a chocolate bribe was going to solve almost a week's worth of worry. To be fair, it did.

Yes it was all true, and my Mum was right, the lady was a 'special dancer'……………and I didn't have to take my clothes off to sing that weekend, or any weekend since actually!

But it did happen that following Saturday evening, you know……..my debut spot at the Piccadilly Club.

Together with floaty pink skirt, sparkly shoes, 'the' sparkly top and one of Mum's necklaces, I did sing on the stage, 'in the big room'. What song was it? Well thanks for asking, it was 'Boom Bang-A-Bang'. And backed by the band it all felt very special.

The past weeks worry just melted away just as quickly as it had arrived.

Where was the chap with the red triangle when you needed him?

Would you have left the office after ten minutes after being told to wait two?

Favourite overheard quote of the time.

"..............Shelley, come and get your dinner, never mind writing about it."

Chapter Two… Oh I Do Like To Be Beside the Seaside

Should you ever find yourself on the east coast of England and at a loose end, treat yourself with a visit to Scarborough. No, I'm not on commission or anything. It's just a nice resort with a lovely beach and some of the finest fish and chips for miles. Walking along the seafront in the evenings is really quite beautiful whatever the season. Having lived and worked in Scarborough in the past I speak from experience.
I've worked at both the Spa and the Futurist Theatres, lovely venues, both overlooking the sea. It's just heartbreaking that the Futurist sadly no longer exists. My story however comes from my residency time at The Grand Hotel, back in the day when it was owned by 'Butlins'. Book Early!

The Grand is quite a breathtaking hotel, which stands proudly on the cliff facing the seafront. You can't miss it, it's the hotel you can see but can never get parked outside of! It really is a stunning building. Built over a hundred and fifty years ago and all designed around the theme of 'time' it has four towers to represent the seasons, twelve floors to mark the months of the year and when it opened in 1867 it had 365 bedrooms, yes, representing the days of the year. These facts are something most 'Reds' (redcoats) learn early on. You are asked about its origin so often by the guests, it's just easier to have the answers. The shape of the hotel was built in the shape of a 'V' in honour of Queen Victoria, luckily she wasn't called Sharon. During a 1940's themed weekend, the main ballroom at the hotel had been transformed into this 40's venue and all the staff, getting into full character, walked around in uniforms and fashions of the day. I got chatting to a guest who told me that in the 1940's she worked at the hotel as a switchboard operator

and that's how she came to meet her husband, he was in the army at the time. She said how when she first began working at the hotel it had the most beautiful wrought iron décor on all the landings. Then she came into work one day to see it all being removed so it could be used for ammunition during the war. The hotels history is absolutely fascinating.
Seriously, I'm not on commission.

I did two stints at The Grand, one in the mid 80's and then it pulled me back again late 1989 for a further 5 years. I fluttered about from redcoat (yay) to band singer, show director and finally to entertainment manager. Making some great friends along the way, we worked hard and played hard and so there is a wealth of stories that come with my time spent there. So what can I tell you that wouldn't warrant a summons landing through the door! Well, in the early days of my time there as a 'red' the hotel was family orientated, I think within a year of working there it changed over to adults only...........Oh, I hope that had nothing to do with my story!
This particular day I'd been asked to cover 'Auntie Red' duties, as the 'reds' that usually did this job were both ill. So together with 'red' Shirley (aka 'Sexy Shirl') we gathered up our collective bundle of kids (32 to be exact) and two by two we marched our way from the hotel down to the beach. Would that even be allowed now? Back then it just seemed like the most natural things in the world to just gather up the kids and take them on the beach for the afternoon, or a ramble. Looking back it was actually ridiculous.
It was mid Summer and the sun was blazing down, yes I'm still talking about the east coast of England. Within minutes of getting there sand castles were being constructed, holes to put water in were being dug, and lots of running towards the sea,

only to run away from it when the tide came in was also popular. Whilst Shirley and I were there to organize games etc, our main job was keeping all the kids in a reasonable enough space so that we didn't lose any. Sorry? What was that? No, no we didn't lose any, so nur nur nur-nur-nur, didn't expect that did you!?

Half way through a rather competitive boy's verses girl's game of Rounders a sad little face came over and stood in front of me. "Oh hello, what's the matter"? I asked. "Do you need the loo? Do you want your Mum? Do you want to play in the team"? Poor little mite just stared at me. Possibly more confused than before he approached me being ambushed with so many questions.

"I want, I want........" he began to answer "I want a pancake"....and his bottom lip dipped and tears filled his eyes.

"Er, you want a pancake"? I repeated back to him. He looked up at me and through emotional stuttering tears said (sniff) "Yes, I wan' wan' want a pa' pancake".

"Well hang on, let's just finish the game and then we'll see yeh?" and he latched himself onto my arm like an extra limb. Soon after this the game did end and the boy's team punched the air and shouted 'we are the champions' whilst jumping up and down and into each other in celebration of their win.

The girls just re-platted their hair stating "well boys are stupid anyway".

I informed Shirley that I had a little boy desperate for a 'pancake' so was going to have a trot along the seafront to see if we could find some, I thought it was possibly a small gimmicky version of one that was being sold, but it was news to me as it was the Shirley, neither having seen or heard of them being sold on the seafront or anywhere else in Scarborough for that matter. However the little lad seemed positive 'he'd had one the day before'. Shirley called to the kids "Did anyone want to go with Auntie Shelley to get something to eat or stay on the beach"?......so I ended up with around 9 kids while the others stayed put with 'Auntie Shirl'.

We walked up to the fairground, and back again..........and up to the fairground, and back again. Not a pancake to be found. "Are you sure you had a pancake yesterday"? I asked the hungry little face.

"Yeh, yeh, my Dad said it was a pancake, he got it from over there", he said wiping his nose on his arm and pointing in a pointy way that kids do, where they point but look in a completely different direction. During this I was constantly on 'kid alert', as one kid would drift away with a promise of sugary food treats we'd all find ourselves waiting in a tight little group until said kid had been served. Then we would gradually move along.

"Are you sure you got a pancake from there"? I asked, my feet protesting at this point and still no sign of a pancake.

All of a sudden the little boy became excited,

"Miss. Look, look, there, the pancake man". And my little pancake eater became very giddy pointing towards to a very brightly painted 'pancake' kiosk. We walked over to the kiosk.

Pancakes? The man didn't have pancakes, but who am I to split hairs over the title of a food stuff, I mean we'd only been plodding up and down the prom for over an hour. Who cares what the pancakes title really was. Well, my poor feet did. We'd actually walked past this kiosk several times, the kiosk that sold.............. donuts. I wonder what his Dad called hot dogs. Baked potatoes!?

With donut stuffed in his 'cakehole' we all trotted back to the beach where Auntie Shirl had got a mass paddling expedition in process. So 'pancakes' in hand, myself and my snack chums all joined in the fun.

After around just short of 4 hours away from the hotel and everyone suitably soaked (come on..........it was never just going to be just paddling in the sea with 32 kids aged between 6 and 13 now was it!) We all got, be it randomly, into our twos again, and just like Noah I led the way back to the hotel with my trail of damp tiddlywinks with Shirl playing anchor at the back. Before leaving the beach we did our headcount with a lot of faffing and fidgety kids, but we counted 32, so all good..............and then reaching the hotel outside the main doors we announced "hang on kids, let's just make sure we're all here".

I began to count "2, 4, 6, 8, keep still please, 10, 12, no, no, please
don't move around to talk to your friends, just wait a moment" I proceeded to walk down the line counting along the way...."14, 16, 18"............"I've lost my socks" said one of the kids".

"Are they in your bag"? I asked and carried on "20, 22, 24".........
"I've got 'em" said the little voice "they were in my pocket". I carried on "26, 28".............. "I want a wee" said another little voice. "Well hang on 2 minutes" I said still counting. "I want a wee as well" said yet another little voice. It became contagious, a little like yawning.

"I re-a-lly need to go now" said the little voice again.

"Just hang on, hang on, won't be long now" I said hurrying down the line. This wasn't unlike the Sooty Show! Almost there........"30, 32, 34, 36"? Uh, that can't be right I thought and looked over at Shirley.

"What's up" she called.

"We definitely went down to the beach with 32 didn't we"? I called.

"Yeh, why"? She answered.

"Well, I've just counted 36"!

"Eh" she laughed, "I bet it's 'cos they won't keep still. Here, you go to the front of the line and I'll count 'em".

"2, 4, 6, 8" she said tapping the munchkins on top of their heads as she wound her way down the queue of now impatient children ……….."28, 30, 32, 34, 36…….oh heck Shell, how's that happened, ya right, there are 36".

"Got an idea" I said to Shirley. "Just need to get them to quiet down".

"Right kids, can you be quiet while Auntie Shelley asks ya something" called out Shirley.

"OK" I started "can you put your hands up if you DIDN'T walk down to the beach with us". My obvious theory being the four extra we accumulated must be our guests and have just joined the fun and games on the beach due to recognizing myself and Shirley. So just after I announced this, four little hands went up right in the middle of the herd,

"Shirley, it's ok" I called, "found 'em, right, the rest can go in", and with that Shirley escorted the others into the hotel through the main doors.

"Hello" I said to the mini hitch-hikers, "come on then" and we also entered the hotel.

"Do you know your room numbers so I can check in with your parents" I asked the tiny faces.

"No" said the tallest of the foursome.

"Alright" I said "well not to worry, but I do need to inform your parents you've been down on the beach with us all afternoon, they must be worried sick. Come on follow me", and I led them to the reception desk.

"What's your sir-name then"? I asked with one of the hotels receptionists poised and ready to spring into action.

"Mason" said the tallest girl. "And are you the eldest sweetie"? I asked.

"Yes" she replied "my names Amber".

"OK Amber, best we let your parents know eh, and are these your sisters and brother"?

"Yeh" she said..........the receptionist came back "Er, we don't appear to have anything on the system in the name Mason, I'll just double check".

"How old are you Amber" I asked "9" came back my reply.

...."and that's Luke and that's..............

And our receptionist came back. "Any luck Adrienne"? I asked.

"No, nothing, I've checked twice, I can't find anything under that name. It doesn't look like their staying here ya know".

"Amber" I said bending down "Is it possible Mum and Dad, or the family member you're on holiday with have booked into the hotel under a different sir-name to you"?

"I don't think so" she said "but were not staying here, and she isn't my sister, we don't know her" she said pointing to the little red head who'd been standing quietly.

What! Did I just hear that correctly?

Not only have we adopted 4 extra children to our kids afternoon on the beach, it's now kidnap. They're not even staying at our hotel, and one of them isn't even related to the other three.

'Don't panic Mr.Mannering'!

"Oohhh hang on" I said "so you're not even staying here", and as I said this the youngest one began to cry.

"Oh it's alright flower" I said trying to comfort the little girl, "we'll get all of this sorted out, there's no need to cry, so what's your name sweetie"? I asked the little red head.

"Suzanne, I'm with my Grandma and Grandad", she said.

"And do you know where you're staying? Is it here?" I enquired.

"It's there" and she pointed across the road to the St. Nicholas Hotel. It appeared Suzanne wasn't even at the beach with us, she had just wandered across the road and joined us while we were

22

all outside (I guess it was quite rowdy and exciting! Well, what can I say Shirl and I knew how to party!).

"You've got your hands full there" said the receptionist.

"Yeh, but at least I know where this one needs to be, can you just let the duty manager know about these three while I take this little one back please"

And with that I ventured across the road to the St. Nick with Suzanne. As we walked through the doors into the reception area there stood her grandparents, absolutely panic stricken, and then in an about turn of seconds were full of love towards their little gem and showering her with hugs and love.

"Oh thank you for getting her back love ", said the elderly lady "Now don't go off like that again, I was worried sick" she said to her granddaughter.

I did a basic background story on what had happened and then left. They were just very grateful their granddaughter had been returned safely and in one piece.

"Ow ya'v got to have eyes in the back of ya head with kids 'aven't ya", said the granddad as we said our goodbyes. I couldn't agree more.

One down, three to go.

In the 10 minutes it had taken me to do this 'return to sender' delivery, our receptionist, as promised had called the duty manager who had taken our three amigos into the café and gave them all drinks and cake while we waited for the police, as in, the real police. No Sting tributes to see here.

"How have you managed to go down to the beach with 32 kids and come back with 36"? he asked, tutting.

"I don't know? a gift"? I sarcastically replied.

"Well" he carried on "I could've understood it if you'd have left with 32 and come back with 30, but an extra 4, ha ha, that's mad"...and he continued to tut, then sniggered his way through his drink, almost like it would've been more acceptable to have 'downsized' the group by accident.

I sat down. "Can you remember the name of the hotel or Bed and Breakfast where you're staying Amber"? I asked looking at the children.

"No, we only got 'ere this morning, n' after we'd unpacked we went to the slot machines an' me Mam left us at the beach after we got to the hotel and then we wanted to join in with the g, g, g, games an' an' and..........." And then she began to cry.........with her siblings looking on.

"No, no, don't cry, listen all of you, we'll get this sorted, don't worry" I confirmed.

Soon after this the police arrived in the form of male and female officers, and I explained the afternoon's drama. They also remarked on how they'd been involved in the losing of kids from group situations, but never adding to. Well, nice to be different isn't it.

"Why did your Mother leave you on the beach? Where is she now, do you have any idea"? Asked the male police officer.

"She went for chips", said the little boy.

"So, she went to get you all chips, and you wandered off to play"? The policeman continued.

"No", said Amber, "she gave us £2 each and said she was going for chips and she'd see us on the beach in half an hour".

"And what time would that have been at"? he continued.

"Er, about half past two I think?", she replied. The time was now approaching 6.30pm.

"Alright then" said the kindly policeman "I think the first thing we should do is just get ourselves down onto the front again and see if we can find your Mother, it's quite possible she's down there looking for you".

"Best if you come along too" he said looking at me. So we all left our table and proceeded to the main hotel exit.

Our cabaret for the evening, Dick Van Winkle, was just arriving through the main doors as I was leaving with 3 kids and 2 police officers.

"Hello……….Ohhh?………..I won't ask" said Dick "just another day in the life of Shelley is it"?

"Something like that, I'll see you later" I said as we all walked down the steps and together with the kids we all got into the police car.

Less than a minute and we were down at the seafront and out of the car, kids glancing up and down the road looking for their Mum.

Ten minutes passed, as did another 10, and another, and…………..

The time crept up to just after 7.30pm. Just as I'd been walking up and down the prom during the afternoon searching for donuts, we were now walking up and down on the hunt for parents.

Every now and again the 'cccchhhh' noise of the police officers radios would blast and they'd talk back to the voice at the other end.

All of a sudden a very dodgy looking bloke rushed over the road to us and mouthed very loud so that everyone in the surrounding area could hear "Amb's where the b……y 'ell have you been eh", and he reached out trying to grab hold of the young girl.

"Hang on just a moment sir" said the police "I take it you know this young girl"?

"Course I do, it's Amber me daughter, well, me girlfriend's lass"……

It all went downhill for me after that.

The loving reunion I'd witnessed at the St. Nick hotel with the grandparents hadn't gone exactly the same way with this reunion.

No sooner had 'the bloke' explained who he was to the police, an irate woman staggered across the road to retrieve her kids. Picture the exact opposite to the reunion of The Railway Children with their father and you've got it. ☹

No loving hugs or kind words………..just noise.

I said my goodbyes to the kids, thanked the police (who were going nowhere fast) and then began to trudge my way back up to the hotel where tears ran down my face for most of the way. You see the Disney ending I'd hoped for didn't happen.

Arriving back at the hotel, I felt quite deflated, so I grabbed a coffee and bent Shirley's ear filling her in with the rest of the story. During this time, I'd also checked in with the duty manager to let him know the outcome.

I went to my room, got refreshed and then back downstairs where I went back stage to the dressing room to get ready for the show opener. I was going to sing a song whilst Shirley and Carol (hiya hen!) did a dance routine you see. While we were getting ready a knock came at the door and there stood Mr. Winkles (aka Dick Van Winkle) asking if I had a black eye pencil (as in the colour black…….not a pencil that gave black eyes! Thought I'd better explain that). He needed one to colour in his mustache! Well, that was a new one on me. I'd never heard that before. As it turned out, I did, so he could.

The cabaret began so after our opening number I stayed on the stage to introduce Mr. Van Winkle, and after his first instrumental on the clarinet (he was a fab multi-instrumentalist you see, sadly no longer with us) he said over the mic,

"Thank you for that lovely introduction Shelley, and nice to see the police released you in good time to do the show"!!!

And without any further explanation he left it at that. Goodness knows what the audience thought. ☺

It was the first time I'd been in a police car and I have no desire to be in one again. Over and out.

I lived in the hotel at this time on the top floor in one of the towers and the following day I woke up to George tapping on my window (George the seagull that is). He would tap away at my window most mornings until I got up and fed him. I'd just finished feeding him when there was a rat-a-tat-tat...........at my door this time. It was Sexy Shirl with an offer I couldn't refuse. "Come on you" she said "we've got a day off, we're gonna go into town for a coffee but before that I'm going to cut ya hair for ya. I know all that with the kids yesterday upset you so I'm going to cheer you up".
She did that alright, we had a great day, and my new hair looked lovely.
Later on that day I had a little surprise visit from Suzanne and her grandparents. They popped over the road to the hotel with a bunch of posies for me. I felt as if I was taking the blooms under false pretences, but they were eager I should have them as a thank you, how kind. I guess all's well that end's well.

I got lost in the Co-Op once as a small child. When my Mum found me it was like we'd been apart for days, weeks even, when it was probably less than 5 minutes. The fuss and love I received on being found was in abundance. I'm thankful my parents belonged to me.

Ever been lost............and then found?

Favourite overheard quote of the time.

"...........excuse me, I've fiddled with the switch thingy but my husband's at home and I'm here with my sister, she's in a different room so can you send a man up!"

Chapter Three... You Can Leave Your Hat On

Losing a parent has to be one of the most traumatic things any one of us has to go through. No lessons at school to teach you how to deal with that now is there. You're left with not only upset, sometimes anger, emptiness, and overwhelming sadness, but also a real physical pain. It's possible to be surrounded by a hundred people and yet you still feel alone. Having lost both my parents I struggle with the term 'time heals'. I think time re-educates your brain on how to cope in the coming weeks, months, years. Heal? I'm not so sure.

My dear Mum left us in the year 1990, and my Dad in 2005. Mum had been ill for some time unknown to many, myself included. She'd decided to deal with her illness privately only telling two people and battle on regardless. Dad however had a relatively short illness, taking ill in the January and then he sadly passed away in the March of the same year. I remember sitting in my garden with the nippy March air blowing around me as I sat thinking "this isn't how it was s'posed to happen". You see in my mind I hadn't 'arranged' things so that they happened like this. In my sparkly fluffy world that I'd created in my head both parents should have been in my life until 'I' was well into my 60's or even beyond that. Sadly it didn't play out like that.

When I was 7 and at junior school my friend Jill was taken out of class one day. The headmistress came in half way through a lesson, whispered something to our teacher and then the teacher walked over to Jill and with a few words escorted her out of the class. We, the class all sat there looking at each other in silence. It was only when we realized Jill was the only one that had been singled out and that the rest of us needn't worry about being taken out of class to face goodness knows what, that the silence cracked and within minutes of this realization bits of paper were being flicked about by rulers and boys were performing mock fighting to impress the girls.

Jill didn't come back into class for the rest of the day, or that week actually. I just couldn't understand it, I mean, she didn't look ill? That same day when I was back at home my Mum, who could've easily been described as a fuss pot whenever I'd returned from school, was rather somber. She sat me down and told me that the reason Jill had been taken out of school that day was that her brother had died. It was a huge shock. Her brother wasn't 'old', he was a teenager, 14 to be precise, and it totally threw me, because now there was a chance of 'anyone' being able to just die. This was something I'd never realized before. Why would I? At age seven I thought dying was the thing only really old people did. I'd also told myself that my parents would always, as in forever, be around. So, all this information came as a terrible shock for a small person.

For weeks following this I constantly had nightmares regarding people dying. I don't blame my Mum in any way for telling me about my friend's brother. You can't shield children forever, much as I'm sure every parent would want to. Death is part of life after all. So after this episode 'I decided' that my parents would be around a very long time, it seemed it was the only way I could function. The complex mind of a child, when you're scared to go to sleep in case you wake up and your parents are gone. I think that has to be the first time I experienced anxiety. And I do mean anxiety as opposed to worry. Worry is something I've done since I could walk. At the time I didn't think it had an actual title. I thought of it as 'my tummy doesn't feel right'. For a few months after the initial news of Jill's brother I carried an invisible weight around with me, a big shoulder bag of real life. It was soon after this life changing episode that our class teacher left to have her first child. It seemed so odd that while Jill's brother had gone, this new person had arrived in the world, that old circle of life thing.

There is an opposite for everything, if there's light, there's dark, hot, cold, etc, and so if there's sad, there has to be happy yeh?....... My Mum always insisted that truth was often funnier than fiction, and in some cases she was right.

Like the time she and friend Doris went to the funeral of a mutual friend of theirs.

I just need to fast forward now to the end of that particular day and Mum and Doris arriving back at our house in a stranger's car. My Dad opened the door "Who's that car belong to"? He asked as the car moved away from outside the front of our house.

"Oh that's just Peter and Alison" said my Mum waving them off on their way.

"Who"? Said my Dad, not having the foggiest who Peter and Alison were.

"Peter and Alison, lovely couple aren't they Doris" Mum said as the ladies removed their coats and Doris nodded in agreement.

"Alright" said Dad "I'll try again, how do you know them"?

"Owwww Tony, you won't believe what's happened today, will he Doris?" said Mum, and the ladies chuckled.

This is how the day played out.

They decided to attend the funeral of an old neighbour called Margaret 'Maggie' Wright. On arriving at the crematorium there were three chapels, and at the first one they reached 15 minutes before the service they looked down the list of names at the door and there was a service booked at midday for 'Elizabeth Margaret Wright'.

'Oh good, we're on time', they thought.

"So she was an Elizabeth then" said my Mum.

"Yeh she must have been eh" agreed Doris.

Nothing unusual about that, many people, including my Mum were/are known by their middle name.

Neither of them recognized any of the congregation waiting, but didn't expect to, they knew the neighbour on a chat at the gate basis and had purely gone along to pay their respects.

It was only half way through the service my Mum clicked they were at the wrong funeral!

'This' lady, 'Elizabeth Margaret' that is, had been a school headmistress, had never married and was a member of the WI. Mum's neighbourhood friend 'Margaret' had been married, widowed, married again, had several children and had been a nurse at the city hospital.

As Mum said "we realized it wasn't her when the vicar was going on about all the fantastic trips abroad she'd had, I don't think Maggie had been further than Cleethorpes" she quipped.

"Why didn't you leave then"? Asked my Dad, as the ladies told their tale.

"Well, we were right in the middle of people sitting down n' we didn't like to, did we Doris".....and Doris nodded along.

Mum continued "It was a beautiful service though and her family chose some lovely music".

"Right" said Dad scratching his head "but it still doesn't explain why you don't get back here 'til gone 5".

"No, well what happened was after the service as everyone was walking out this woman's niece was thanking everyone for coming n' I felt awful, well we both felt guilty truth be known, so I stopped and said that 'we shouldn't really have been there, we should've been at our friends funeral but when we realized our mistake we felt rude leaving and that they gave her aunt a lovely send off, nice music, lovely service, and we were both very sorry for their loss as she seemed like a nice lady'. Before we knew what was happening we'd been invited to the wake at the Co-Op rooms and we just thought 'oh go on then' n' this lovely couple in front of us had heard everything and just offered to take us, n' that's all really".

My Dad stood open mouthed, it wasn't the first time and it wasn't the last he'd be speechless regarding some activity Mother had unwittingly found herself in.

While we're on the subject of life and death, don't you find some words can make a situation even worse, and in the theme of our chat the word I speak of is coffin.........it's so...........coffin'y! Bad enough you are going through such a sad time in your life, you also have to deal with this word. I say we change this to a 'Tidybye'. Not being disrespectful, just feeling a softer sounding title would make the planning and send off somewhat gentler. I'll leave you with that one.

So as if the magnitude of losing my Mum wasn't bad enough in late 1990, now my Dad had also gone fifteen years after her. All had not gone to plan. My Dad did achieve something quite rare however, after my Mum he met and married a lady called Teresa, both being successful marriages, one of 31 years and the other 13 years. As a wise man said on the day of Dad's funeral, "...Tony achieved two happy marriage's some people don't even manage one".

The weeks following this sad event every film on TV had happy families in it, everyone walking down the street had a parent at the side of them, and Mother's Day, and Father's Day cards seemed to be on display in the shops for the whole of the Spring and Summer! Of course, none of it happened like that, it just felt that way, I'd had blinkers on and hadn't seen the couple having an argument, the mother telling off the child for misbehaving and the old lady wandering along on her own, and DFS having yet another sale......ahh, it never leaves ya.

However at the time of my Dad leaving us I was working as resident singer with a band in Yorkshire. Six nights a week I would put on the sparkly outfits, slap on the war paint and off onto the stage I would go, singing and chatting to the audience like I didn't have a care in the world. Off stage I had become a little quieter of late. It's true to say, I wasn't really me. But my sleeping pattern was patchy and erratic, and I just really wanted to save my energy for performing. To be honest I believe that the work ethic of 'be bright and cheery' actually saved me from going to a rather 'dark place'. People don't go away on holiday to look at a sad face on the stage, so the routine of 'be bright and cheerful' actually helped me to a certain degree. You know your brain can't distinguish the difference between a real smile and a fake one! So when you smile the brain sends the happy chemicals to your body regardless. Now that's pretty amazing.

Off stage however while I wouldn't be ignorant or rude I knew I had become a very quieter version of 'me'. It went on for longer than I anticipated, and I didn't really know how to shake it off. That old saying I mentioned earlier, 'time heals' wasn't doing as it said on the tin. Shangri La it was not! However, things were about to improve from an unlikely source.

Things start to cheer up now I promise, keep reading.

Now and again I would travel to the gig (which from my home was 15 minutes) with the drummer of the band, Paul, a nice lad, with a very dry sense of humour. We would talk about allsorts on our little journeys, the meaning of life, weather, bicycle clips, you name it we talked about it. He told me once that on inspection of his birth certificate he discovered he was a year younger than he'd always thought. I know! So, yes we covered a wide variety of subjects, well almost everything.

One evening on the way home he approached the subject of my Dad, and I really couldn't say more than a sentence. Not through fear of crying, it was almost as if I didn't know how to string a sentence together regarding that subject. My feelings around that time were so confused and foggy to say the very least. I didn't really know what to say, so I said very little, it was just the easy option in handling it.

The following day I'd been watching a local news programme on TV and there was an item about a new stretch limousine service that had sprung up in the area. Nothing thrilling about that I hear you say. Well, it was a limo service with a difference. This limo company was aimed at hen and stag parties and the chauffeur's would either be rather sexy ladies dressed as bunny girls, aimed at the stags, we presume! Or tanned men with muscles upon muscles that wore very little but a smile and a leopard skin G-string for the hens, 'cluck' 'cluck'! I don't remember what the limo business was called, but it was along the lines of 'Susan's Sexy Limo Service'....a lot of thought had gone in to giving it a title obviously.

Traveling to work that evening Paul and I were chatting about this, we decided between ourselves that the two choices were quite obvious. 'What about the people that would maybe want a fuller figure lady, or a really skinny man', we both ranted, and as we got chatting we came to the conclusion that the possibilities were endless.....our chat went off onto the most crazy, ridiculous path, basically something for everyone.

Paul being of very slim build said to me "well, it's good you think that way, when you get your own business started up, don't forget to put me on ya books". We then went through a whole list of fanciful names for my 'pretend' stretch limo business.

'Shelley's Saucy Limos'.............'Shelley's Stretchy Limo Experience'.........and finally 'Shelley's Bare Ar*e Limos'...(in the Shakespeare'ian sense of course!). Yes, the latter was the winner. I said to Paul, if he didn't mind just wearing just his Y-fronts with a chauffeur's hat and dickie bow then the job was his, classy. It was the most I'd chuckled in months.

Two or three weeks went by and things were pretty much the same with my mind set. I'd busied myself beyond busy over the weeks, now months since my Dad's passing. However there are only so many times you can arrange and re-arrange the inside of cupboards and drawers. I'd run out of furniture! The weekend approaching was a 1970's themed break at the hotel where I sang. I'd said to Paul how I didn't really know what to dress as, and asked him if he'd had any ideas for himself.
"Oh one or two" he replied, keeping his cards very close to his chest.
"Like what" I asked.
"Oh never you mind" he said with a cheeky little smile. Anyhow the Saturday night arrived and approximately two hours before Paul was due to pick me up. I received a text..........'I might be slightly late by 5 minutes, but I will be there, just come out to the car'...........I didn't think any more of it. I remember this so well as I'd just got my first ever mobile phone by a few weeks. I was so late in getting a personal phone and finally succumbed to having one as I was getting left behind. Everyone was chatting away on a little piece of black plastic and I was shaking corn, and calling my pidgeon back! Still pretty much that way now, I mean, 'my' mobile phone runs on gas!
Just before 7pm I got dressed in true 70's fashion, taking on the identity of Agnetha Falkskog (aka, the blonde one from ABBA). Flared trousers, a cheesecloth top, platform shoes, beads, a dinky hat and a full blonde wig helped with the disguise,

yes, that'll do nicely I thought as I checked out my new look in the mirror. As the time approached 7.30pm I vaguely heard music of an ice cream van style outside. Initially I didn't give it much thought until I realized the time and thought "crickey, he's late doing his rounds". I then realized what the tune of the ice cream van actually was, and it certainly wasn't 'Popeye the Sailor Man'.

Grabbing my bag and locking the door behind me I could hear the 'ice cream van' music tinkling away, rather loudly, it was then I realized it was…….. 'I'm Too Sexy' (for my shirt)! As I walked around the side of my house the little red car I was familiar with wasn't parked up, instead I was met with a white boxy estate car, all the windows were down and in the driving seat sat………a half naked man!!!

Walking closer I was very aware of curtains twitching in the cul-de-sac, and I wasn't surprised. There in the estate car sat Paul in the driving seat, chauffeur's hat, black dickie bow, white Y-fronts, and nothing more, with the 'Right Said Fred' classic tinkling away in the mild evening air.

"Shelley's Bare Ar*e Limo's at your service madam" he said, with the straightest of faces.

"Ohhhhhhhhhh my goodness PAUL"! I said.

"What"? He replied, "We talked about this and you were deadly serious, so here I am…..don't say you're not going to give me a job now".

And I laughed and laughed and laughed……..and laughed and laughed.

I stood leaning over onto the car looking through the open window on the passenger side….dressed as Angetha. So yes, nothing new, just a regular Saturday night…… it's no wonder all the curtains were twitching.

"How have, er how come, how, er how........." I stammered and then started laughing again.

As the music swirled around the little cul-de-sac Paul said "Are you getting in then or are you just going to stand there making a show of yourself". Yes, because that's what was odd here!!!

I got in the car and with Paul staying in character and with music playing we reversed, and then slowly........everso slowly.......so slowly in fact a man walking his dog over took us........drove up the little drive onto the main road. Did we get some strange looks? that would be a yes! Each and every time we came to a junction where we had to stop we got some very odd glares indeed. I just laughed and laughed and laughed. On the last stretch to the hotel there was a lovely country pub with seating outside, it was right next to a junction. As stated it was a mild evening and lots of people were sitting outside enjoying their drinks. We had to stop at this junction to let the traffic pass by. I don't think the punters could believe exactly what they were witnessing, and maybe went home after we'd moved on thinking they'd probably had too much to drink already.

Arriving at the hotel and parking up, still laughing, I asked Paul 'where had the car come from'?

He said "well mine has got a few bits n' bobs that need sorting and it has to go through its MOT next week, so I've had to leave it at the garage and I needed a car for this weekend and I just bought this 'run-a-round' to tide me over till I get my own car back instead of hiring one".

I think there may have been a little more thought into it than just that! The cars saucy jingle for a start. I for one have never heard that tune in the style of an ice cream van before, have you? Also the chauffeur's hat! Where did that come from? Not like we all have one just hanging about in the house is it? He'd gone to all that trouble, just for me! How kind and thoughtful was that.

I got out of the car and he said "I'll be there in five minutes, I think its best if I put some clothes on before I come into the hotel"....and I carried on laughing, in fact I could hardly get up the steps into the building for laughing.

I eventually made my way into the hotel and through the door to the back stage area where 70's band 'The Rubbettes' were loitering! (They were the guest star band for the evening). I was 'still' laughing. One of them said "Oh, someone's very cheerful" I didn't know any of them as I hadn't worked with them before this, but that aside I was eager to tell them what I'd just experienced and they all stood there just looking at me rather confused. Paul then walked through the door looking relatively 'normal' as I said "Him, its him, that's who I was telling you about, here he is, it's him...hee hee hee him, he was the one that did it, the hat, the car, hee hee hee"........and I realized, actually, I'm standing here dressed as the blonde from ABBA, rattling on about a friend who turned up wearing his underpants and driving a car with the music to 'I'm Too Sexy' playing in tinkly tinkly fashion, and Paul is standing there not saying a word in quite sedate day to day 70's clothing. Not sure to this day if they believed me.

For the rest of the evening each time I passed the visiting cabaret room where our visiting acts would congregate, or one of The Rubettes passed the band room and saw me they just pointed and said "she's strange that one". And I laughed and laughed and laughed.

It was a fantastic night. It began so bizarrely and was totally out of the norm. The audience being so appreciative and lively, and from start to finish the dance floor was full. Being on stage with the band, well, it was just so enjoyable followed by 'The

Rubbettes', and what a nice bunch of chaps and great 'live' band they turned out to be, their vocal harmonies being second to none.

Yes, such a great night, but it was also the night I made a huge faux pas regarding a couple of guests. I recognized the gent in question as he really looked after himself and was quite a handsome man in his mid to late 50's, so he kinda stood out in a crowd. I walked over and spotting his (presuming wife/girlfriend) lady with him I said,

"Hello, so your back again" (looking at 'her' now) "oww I like your hair, not that the blonde didn't suit you, but this auburn is a lovely shade, it looks really nice".

There seemed a long uncomfortable silence. The woman was glaring at the man and the man was looking at the table, and that's when I realized, 'ahhh yes, this man 'was' here a few weeks ago, but he was with a different lady'.

I could feel the colour rising up my neck and face..........is it me or is it hot!

I then said "Oh ya know what, I've got you mixed up with Dave and Helen (who? I have no idea). You (I said looking at the chap, and isn't it a good thing I didn't actually know his name!) look so much like Dave, they were here a few weeks ago, and Helen (good old Helen) is always changing the colour of her hair. Ow sorry, what must you think of me. Anyhow both of you enjoy the rest of the evening. I'll come back and get to know you once I've taken my foot out of my mouth". I ended it with a laugh, as did they, and I could see the relief coming over the gents face.

As I was singing the following evening, they were having a smooch on the dance floor and so everything must have been back on track. The same evening during cabaret time I went to the bar for a coffee and the gentleman approached me.

"Thank you for last night" he said,

"Oh you're welcome" I replied, hoping no one within earshot had actually heard the conversation!!!

"Between us we managed to convince my 'friend' that I hadn't been here before" he smiled rather sheepishly.

I then felt I let the sisterhood down as I said,

"Well, you do what you have to do, if it makes you happy etc. But a bit of advice, go to different hotels, you will get recognized and it won't be pleasant for you if it happens again and you can't wiggle your way out of it".

"Yes, your probably right" said the well groomed, well spoken gent.

He thanked me again and then walked from the bar back to his date.

He seemed like a nice man, and I didn't know his circumstances, so who was I to judge, plus I was right in the middle of a 'life is too short' episode, so was feeling generous. But even years later on, I do hope that man was as nice as I thought he was.

Going home I told Paul all about the Casanova in the hotel and how I'd put my foot in it, which Paul found very amusing. As we chatted there were no tinkly tunes being played, and a distinct lack of Y-fronts on show, but I laughed so much. That evening I definitely turned a corner. My resistance of 'enjoying myself without feeling guilty about it' since my Dad passing had certainly been addressed. The mad thing about that is my Dad, and Mum for that matter loved having fun, loved the daft side of life and would always be in the centre of anything that involved giggles, if not creating them in the first place. I guess grief can take us to places in our heads that we didn't even know existed, and we as 'humans' just need to be helped back onto the right path now and again.

I will never forget that night. It was so obscure how could I. And I'll never forget the effort and time Paul went to in making it so special. Some people you don't meet by accident, they are placed there strategically at the right place at the right time.

Putting aside the car journeys that I had on several occasions where the sun roof leaked so bad that when it rained you'd have to have an umbrella up 'in' the car....really........then the 'limo' car journey was the most crazy road experience I've ever had.
Keep your eyes open for that stretch limo service in the future.
Well.........you never know!!!

So, what's the strangest journey you've ever had?

Favourite overheard quote of the time...

"........after he said 'bum' on stage I thought well, it could go either way tonight."

Chapter Four... Hello

During a touring show and staying in a Travel Lodge hotel, I was pottering about. Hang on...........pottering about.........discuss. Where does this term come from? Pottering about......never in the history of my 'pottering about' have I ever pottered anything, and apart from school years I've never been within sneezing distance of a potter's wheel.........I'm glad we've cleared that up!

So you may be thinking 'how could she potter about in a travel lodge room'. Well, it may just be a travel lodge room to you, but to me, another little home. So those that know me and have toured with me will know I don't just arrive at a travel lodge. I settle! So together with my regular luggage, after unpacking, I would clean the room. Yes, clean the room, even though I could see it was clean, (well, all apart from a rather unpleasant stay near Biggleswade) I needed to c-l-e-a-n. I s'pose this is a bit like a cat or dog marking their territory. I would then get out the cushions and throw, put the kettle on, get the latte out and only 'then' could I relax. You may think 'what a waste of energy'. But living out of a suitcase as many that do so will tell you, it can be hard. So those little touches of home comforts, well you'd be surprised how much it helps, such a tiny thing that can have such a big impact. Maybe that's why on a particular tour with a cast of six, three girlie-girls and three gentle-boys my room would always be the one that was magnet like, and my fellow artistes would coo at my cushions, thrill towards my throws and be regular visitors to my nest. No manic gatherings, more sophisticated soirees.

After the first six weeks of the first tour I ever did, I would write down what town/city I was in. So on waking up in the morning there would be my little note to myself to remind me I was in Maidenhead or wherever it may be. It just made the first five minutes of wake-up time easier recognition. You see one place can look pretty much like the next. Our city and town centres with many of the same shop chains can be carbon copies of each other and can play havoc with your whereabouts when you're on the move. Edinburgh and York you have no need to worry, I know there are other exceptions to the rule, but I'm speaking of majority. I have to say travel lodge wise in my experience, Scotland have the ones that have the most individuality, which makes it so much easier to register where you are than just glancing over the tour sheet.

Before the days of the travel lodge I decided a treat was in order for my Mum. It came in the form of two nights in a hotel in London, which came complete with a nice meal, Cliff Richard in concert and a plod about playing the tourist. Before any of that happened however we had to get to London, so wanting to make the experience fabulously spoilt from start to finish, I'd pre booked train tickets and also taxi's to and from the station. On the way to the station our taxi pulled up, Mum and I got inside and Dad waved us off at the door, and a bit excited Mum duel waved at Dad whilst saying 'hello' to the driver. The taxi driver wasn't over chatty but was friendly enough. He had the radio on in the car and I noticed that the chap being interviewed was quiz show host Bob Holness. Bob was chatting about being the first James Bond. Serious James Bond fans will know this to be true as Bob played 007 on the radio. Well knowing my Mum had been to Central TV on a few occasions to watch the filming of 'Blockbusters' and knowing how she liked Mr. Holness I nudged her arm in the back of the cab and gesturing towards the front of the car (i.e. radio) I half whispered,
"Mum…………it's Bob Holness"

"Is iiiiiiit"? she replied.

"Yes" I said, a little surprised by her over enthusiastic interest. All three of us then sat in silence as our journey continued. We were about half way to the station in town when we approached traffic lights that had just changed to red.

All of a sudden as the car drew to a halt my Mum leaned forward and grabbing hold of the shoulders of the driver sitting in front of her said,

"Oh I say duckie, I am surprised you're havin' to do a second job, don't the tele pay you so well then"

"MUM"!!! I said "what are you doing"?

"Oh don't be daft you, no need to get all embarrassed, I'm just chatting to Bob" she said,

"Eh?...........Mum! 'that' isn't Bob Holness! 'He's' on the radio" I squirmed.

"OOOOooooooopppppppp" she loudly whooped.

"Owww I am a daft begger" she said as she continued to keep hold of the driver!

"I thought it was a bit daft he was doing Blockbusters and having a taxi job, oww in't it funny how ya mind works".

Fortunately while he wasn't the chattiest chap he did have a sense of humour and laughed all the way to the station. As it happens it was the start of a lovely little break.

Are you familiar with the movie 'Young at Heart'? Doris Day, Frank 'blue eyes' Sinatra, lovely film. Everything you require for a rainy Sunday afternoon. Doris Day, nice music, cute dog, stylish frocks and pretty blossom tree lined streets. However towards the end of the film it goes rather bleak, as Mr. Sinatra, as the character Barney Sloan finds himself at the wheel of a car and turns off the windscreen wipers whilst driving with the heavy snow coming towards him. Well I was touring with a band in Germany during winter and that sort of happened to us, except our driver had the wipers going on the fastest speed possible and yet we still we couldn't see out of the window. Pulling over to the side of the road, we think? (To be honest we could've been in the middle of a field, the weather was so bad) within ten minutes of stopping we suddenly heard banging on the side of the mini bus.

"Guten tag" "Guten tag" "Hallo, HALLO" It was the police. Our driver (who spoke no German) was trying to explain to the police (who spoke no English) why he'd pulled over. It got slightly heated, for no other reason other than the language barrier. They insisted one of the police officers would drive our mini-bus, and we were followed by the police car...............to a prison. Once we got there, an English speaking officer came to our aid and explained the weather was so bad we'd be risking our lives to go on, so for the night we would have to stay at the prison. That has to be the longest night of my life. I didn't sleep at all. Yes we were in an empty block where no male prisoners were, and yes I had a 2 bunk cell all to myself, it just felt very uncomfortable. Trying to conjure up jolly thoughts of the comedy 'Porridge' had very little effect on relaxing me. You try and go to the loo when you can hear men calling like rowdy parakeets down the corridor, I don't know if it was better or worse that I couldn't understand what they were saying, I just remember begging the guitarist of our band to "please come to the loo with me and wait outside on guard". That night I slept...................well...........slept?...not really........with one eye open, it was like nothing I've ever experienced. I think that one time in prison was plenty. Well, I don't like to be greedy. The following day we were off on our travels again as the weather had calmed down during the early hours. The things we do for our art.

Free the Nottingham one!!!

I now whisk you eighteen months on and I was staying at Stoke on Trent and had a craving for egg on toast, so ventured into the town and sourced a café. Handy in that it wasn't too far from the venue where we were performing. As I walked in a couple were just leaving which just left myself and a man sitting in the far corner. I ordered my meal and sat down, he looked over at me, and I smiled at him........he smiled back. We then spent the next 40 minutes batting over the room to each other a wink, a smile, a nod, all very friendly. I felt as if I should know him, but as I didn't really know anyone that lived in Stoke back then (to my knowledge that is) I didn't give it much more thought. As I finished my meal he stood and acknowledged the lady serving and walked towards the door, on his travels out of the café he stopped at my table smiled, leaned over and said in a hushed voice, "Hello dear, so nice to see you again, I'll leave you to get on with your coffee, take care".
I said "Euuhhhhhiii", smiled, and he left.
The lady walked over to my table and picking up my plate said "everything alright for you love"
I said "yes very nice, thank you. Could you tell me, do you know the man that just left? He appeared to know me".
She said "Oh that's Frankie Howerd he's doing a panto down the road, he's in here most days".
Well, maybe with hindsight I should have corrected him by saying "I'm not who you think I am, ney, ney and thrice ney".......Oww titter ye not! But I didn't.
Oh!!! This does happen to me from time to time people assuming I'm someone else. I'm just wondering if the real version of who people presume I am is walking about with people calling to her

over the road "Shelley, how are you"! (*wonders* do you s'pose she'd like to take on my ironing?)

I'm guilty for speaking to people I don't know, many people actually. If someone smiles at me, I'm in, and can strike up a conversation at the drop of a hat. I hold doors open and let streams of people walk through smiling at them and saying "hello", "hi" "morning" "hello there". I've always thought this is a combination of my upbringing and also the work I did in my formative years. But it happens to this day, I can stand for quite some time holding doors for folk, and this has nothing to do with work. This is standing at the doors leading into Debenhams! It instantly takes me back to my first season away and the day after getting home I'd had a trip into the city centre with Mum and as they say old habits die hard. I opened the door for Mum to go through, saw a lady heading towards me and just stood there holding the door for her, giving out smiles and 'hellos' to anyone else that needed door assistance. That was until my Mum realizing I hadn't followed her, came back and said "what are you doing"? I honestly hadn't realized I'd stood there for so long. It was just something you did as a 'coat' so was second nature to me. Talking about this to fellow 'coats' since, it was unanimous "yeh, been there, DO that". It's something I still do do! (do, doo do doo doo, fancy a sing-song anyone?)

I got chatting to a lady in the doctor's waiting room some years ago, and she said that she lived alone with no family to speak of, so if she walked to her village in the morning and someone smiled and said good morning to her it could set her up nicely for the rest of the day. How lovely and how sad, I've never forgotten that conversation, I think it has affected me, in a positive sense, ever since. Pass a smile on, it could change someone's day for the better.

Standing outside the Arts Theatre after a meeting in Nottingham in 1984 and waiting for a taxi. It was throwing it down with rain. There was a poor chap who looked slightly older than me a few steps away from me getting soaked so I asked "Excuse me, hello, would you like to share my umbrella" he did indeed. We got chatting and he told me his name was Howard. I'd never met anyone like him, and haven't since in all honesty. We shared the taxi and he was so charismatic with a hint of hippy. Oww, and really friendly teeth. How do I explain that?............I don't think I can...........they were just so lovely, naturally white, lovely shaped, and he had a lovely laugh.
Whoa, steady, I know what you're thinking there. No.........I was already with a cute boyfriend, waiting for me in the wings and didn't really want another. As my Dad used to say, "Ow's courting ya know".
Howard was a really nice young man though and due to my offer of shelter and share of a cab, we exchanged numbers and we became pals. A couple of weeks after our brolly-toots-sweet meet we arranged a little coffee getting to know you time in the city centre. The chat went through a two way zig-zag of information over a steady stream of 6 coffees........yes, six. I've never forgotten that as at the time I'd never drank so much coffee in one sitting. Our chatter time, which covered family and friends, interests and what we did for a living was all very casual and easy like we'd known each other years. It was during this he offered me a string of half a dozen gigs in and around Lincoln. He was setting up an extra's acting agency with his brother and due to this had connections with a few hotels requiring singers for

events. I couldn't believe it. You see, you never know who you're talking to, so those good manners paid off.
As it states in a song I wrote.

"You will find, being kind, is very beneficial to your state of mind"

The last I heard of this lovely man was his business was going from strength to strength and that after a short move to London he moved to California.

In the late 1990's and the early noughties I lived in Harrogate. On the way home one Friday afternoon after performing at an event in Skipton, my husband and I (hold that thought!) were driving through Harrogate and I remarked,
"Isn't it quiet for a Friday afternoon? I haven't seen one car on the road yet".
He agreed, but we didn't think any more about it. As we drove down through the town centre I noticed people lining either side of the road,
"Oh look" I said "something must be happening later, look at all these people".
The said people looked at us blankly as we continued to tootle down the road past the on-lookers who were giving our solitary car some odd looks.
"Something 'must' be going on today" I continued "but I haven't heard anything, have you"?
"No, nothing that I'm aware of" came back his reply.
It was a glorious sunny day and so we came to the conclusion that the sunshine had brought out the crowds, we ourselves had the windows down and sun roof open.
We carried on and as we approached the entrance to the walk way of the town centre the traffic lights turned to red and so we stopped. We were right outside Betty's Tea Shop – the

famous tea café – there were around half a dozen people outside the shops doorway, positioned as if they had just come out of the establishment. Closest to the car was an elderly lady, but very smartly dressed. She turned looked directly at me. I smiled. She smiled back and continued to look at me. At this point in my life I worked as a resident singer in a hotel in the area. Each week I would be faced with 800 plus guests, and more often than not I would be walking through the town during the day and hear someone call my name with a cheery 'hello'. I confess nine times out of ten I didn't always know who the person was, but later on in the evening, I would often have couples dance by the stage and call to me "saw you today in town, you looked very busy". It's far easier for 800 to recognize one person, than the other way around.

Figuring this elderly lady must be a guest who 'belonged to the hotel' and not wanting to appear ignorant, I waved out of the window and called,

"Woohoo hello duckie" and continued to wave.

She smiled again, gave a little gentle wave back. My husband said, "Who are you waving at". So I said,

"Oh one of the oldies from the hotel", and with that I gave another little bouncy wave and a, "byeeee duckie, byeeee" as the lights changed to green and we slowly moved away the husband said,

"Ya daft thing, what if it wasn't one of the guests from the hotel, you've just waved and called out to a complete stranger".

I said "Well it doesn't really matter does it, not like I was being rude, it was all friendly and……."…………….and it was in that moment that I suddenly realized who the well dressed old dear was. It was only herself……….HRH, The Queen.

"OHHHHHHhhhhhhhhhhh it was the Queen, the actual Queen, our countries Queen, the Queen that lives in London, THE Queen" I said, seriously confirming who the genteel lady was. After the initial shock and reality of what had just happened, my husband said,

"Where on earth is her security"? Good question.

Sure enough on the local news item that evening we saw the Queen and Prince Philip strolling out of 'Betty's' with some voice over talking about how the area had felt it an honour to welcome the royals to the town on such a beautiful day, and as the camera panned out as clear as day there was our little car making its way down the hill. Bonkers!

Arriving home it did make me laugh, I just wasn't expecting to see 'the' Queen, well....you don't, do you.

I was raised with good manners thankfully, Mum would've been proud. I'd love to know what the Queen made of it.................possibly....

"Philip, who was that giddy woman waving franticly out of the car. One doesn't recall the face"? Or did one?

And as friends said to me that evening after telling them about my close encounter during the afternoon,

"Isn't it a good thing it was you that was so close to her without any apparent protection around her"...........Umm isn't it just.

I would have loved to have been a fly on the wall at the security re-assessment that evening. I think someone may have had their legs smacked.

A popular misconception about the world of show business is that it's glamorous. The glamorous side of it is probably 25% the rest is hard work. Strange how often the public's perception of working in showbiz isn't that of real work. No wonder the TV talent shows which conjure up a life of sparkles and fantasy attract thousands upon thousands ready to audition looking for that chance of a lifetime of living the dream, many falling at the first hurdle. It's hard work, and it's only the people at the very top get to live the ultimate dream lifestyle.

During my very first season, time and time again after working your socks off and entertaining at every available opportunity the guests would say "Ohhhh hello love, we've really enjoyed it, you do work hard. So what's your proper job"? Uh.

This is only to be pipped at the post by friends who work on the cruise lines who are constantly asked by the entertained passengers "Do you go home at night?"

And their answer "Well.........no actually we don't". Put that in ya pipe and smoke it.

Okay, you've cornered me, there are glamorous times, of course there are. With that much glitter and sequin activity how could there not be? And there are the exciting times. Example, I did a matinee show in Southend at the Cliffs Pavilion Theatre, directly after the show I jumped into a taxi where I was rushed to The London Palladium to do the evening show, now that was rather exciting, and nice posh frocks to be worn on both occasions so......

This too-ing n fro-ing between shows has happened to me on quite a few occasions over the years. Not a complaint at all, even though on several occasions I was practically meeting myself on the way back, always thoroughly enjoyable. Once I did a matinee at Crewe Lyceum Theatre and afterwards had a taxi journey to central Manchester to do an evening show.

My taxi driver however was not what you'd call the norm. We got stuck in traffic and he looked around into the back of the cab as I was unclipping hair extensions out to re-clip a new look in, and said to me "hello, hello, we've got traffic as far as the eye can see dear lady. I hope you're alright for time"

I replied "Well I should be, I'm doing a show, but it doesn't start until 8pm so as long as I get there for 7pm at the latest....."
No sooner had I said the word 'show', he produced.........a guitar! Yes, 'in' the taxi. He spent the rest of the traffic jam and any red light stops after that, strumming away and singing as I harmonized, well I was hardly just going to sit there was I.
We covered everything from reggae to musical theatre. It was complete and utter madness. Having lived the life I have it wasn't so much shocking as just a little bit unusual being as I was in a taxi. The driver was quite eccentric, so he fit rather nicely into the strange world of the showbiz criteria.

Do you consider any part of your career glamorous?

Favourite overheard quote of the time.......

"...my dentist looks like Gary Wilmot, but I haven't dared ask him if he can sing.........you see if he did it might be rubbish and I'd have to look enthusiastic with him poking about in my mouth."

Chapter Five... Talk To Your Daughter

Putting aside the year or so in the juniors where I was relentlessly bullied by a rather nasty piece of work and her older sisters, I quite liked school. Well, when I say I liked school, maybe I should have been a little clearer on that, as in, I liked art lessons, dancing, drama, music and my pals.

So, junior school, yeh, I really have mixed feelings regarding my memories. What should have been a totally stress free time of learning and making friends, plus pocket money on a Friday of course, was poisoned with this fear of being verbally or physically picked on day to day. It wasn't the best of times for me it has to be said. However, it came to an abrupt end when 'she – the bully' decided she was going to 'give me a pasting' after school one day. Well, we were about 14 months on from the first time she decided I was her chosen interest of hate, and quite frankly I couldn't put up with another 14 minutes of it let alone another 14 months, so as she moved towards me with her nostrils flaring ready to give me another pounding cheered on by her sisters, I punched her.........just the once, Oops! It knocked her off balance. She gracefully fell backwards and then on the floor with her feet bouncing up into the air after her, had it not been under such fraught circumstances it would have been funny. As she sat on the pavement there was look of shock on her face. Her sisters ran off, and she just dragged herself up and backed off growling at me "YOU'LL BE SORRY".

No, I wasn't actually! I didn't know if it would end the reign of terror that welcomed me every single school day or it would actually lead to that pasting, what I did know was that I needed to own up and tell my Mum. So reaching home, I did just that. "Er, I've hit someone, I didn't want to but............." I said, and a potted but concise version of the bullying came out.

My poor Mothers face as I explained I'd been bullied for, well, far too long. Her maternal instinct possibly screaming inside "why didn't I notice this was happening". But you don't allow it to show, that's a sign of weakness isn't it? Isn't it? Well I thought it was, so pushed on regardless, more fool me. I should have said something earlier, but the threat of things getting worse was always promised, so...........I just didn't.

The following day Mum went into school with me, 'the bully' was summoned to the headmaster's room as were her accomplices, and 'her' Mother. We all stood in the office while I had to explain my actions. I don't know what the headmaster was about to say after that, he opened his mouth but the bullies Mother shouted "WHAT HAVE I TOLD YOU ABOUT 'BLEEP' PICKIN' ON OTHER 'BLEEP' KIDS, YA LITTLE 'BLEEP', scary woman. There followed a scuffle as the headmaster and his assistant attempted to restrain the Mother as she walloped the three siblings with the back of her hand! Talk about teach your children!

The rest of that day at school was rather nice. In my now relaxed state I felt as if I could actually 'enjoy' the lessons, the weight of the world for now was off my shoulders, it was bloomin' lovely. When I walked into the house after school my Auntie Peg was visiting and having been filled in on the story by my Mum, Auntie gave me a reassuring gee-up as she greeted me in the sitting room with the clickety clack of her knitting needles in full speed she said,

"Hello me duck, I hear you've got the bullies sorted then, little so n' so's. *whistle* Eh an' I hear the Mother was a bit loud n' all *whistle* Yeh, I know the sort, mouth sa' big you could get both hands in and still wind wool".............

After that school became 'safe' again. My 'bully' had a personality transplant and didn't mix with or talk to anyone. Her sisters moved to another school, and for a short time in the juniors life was good. I felt as if I'd grown over night! And with all this new found knowledge I felt a lot older than the now smaller children I seemed to be towering over, I knew more than they did, I could see out of the windows without standing on a chair, and if I so wished I felt I could have had the control of the school playground. It didn't last however, as wallop, I found myself in a matter of months at the 'Big School', feeling smaller than ever as an 11 year old first year student, all this plus the extra trauma for me as it was only 3 months previously to leaving the juniors I'd got married!

Yes, John Bradford and I had said 'I do' at the side of the rabbit hutches next to the caretakers house. It will come as no surprise to you that this is one of my most vivid junior school memories the rest is a blur of trips to the park, school plays, being bullied, and having to do P.E. once in my navy blue pants! Is that still allowed to happen in schools? Or like the cane and free milk for all, is it a thing of the past? just askin'.

Meanwhile back at the 'wedding', our mutual school pals Julie Cartledge played vicar and Carol Hurst was our bridesmaid and 'Rusty' the care takers dog was pageboy. I, as bride, wore Carol's dark green 'dress up' gypsy skirt and white gypsy blouse. In our eyes it was a 'real' event and had to be dressed accordingly. I even sang at my own wedding, and John beamed with pride, peeping at me under the hood of his anorak. I figured why get 'a turn' in when I could sing myself for the reception. The reception being the four of us sharing a bag of penny mix sweets. The marriage consisted of John saving me a seat at dinner time, putting his coat over my head if it rained, buying me Polos, and giving me loving looks over the hall at assembly, simple but sweet.

After so many weeks we all had to go our separate ways at the end of term, as it also meant secondary school time.

I never did get that annulment.

Being separated from your friends you'd grown up with, well, it was a nerve wracking experience until we'd settled in a little, got used to the enormity of the building, made new friends and grown accustomed to new teachers.

The first week of secondary school, aka 'Alderman W. Derbyshire Comprehensive', we 'little 'un's' were taken on a tour of the school. By the end of the day I felt as if I'd done a sponsored walk. It was tummy knottingly exciting though. Unlike the juniors where we just had a school hall, this school hall was not only twice the size, but it had a large, as professional as you'd get in a theatre, stage at one end of it, with curtains, lights, the lot. There was also a gym, library, tennis courts and two fields! In the juniors we'd had to go across the road to the park if we wanted to see a blade of grass.......Yep, things sure had changed on Walton's mountain!

Apart from the stage area calling me, the other impressive parts of the tour for me was the art department. The art that hung over our heads and graced the walls as we were escorted into the classes looked like it had been done by famous artistes, the standard was amazing. I later discovered that one of the art teachers was a bit stern (I'm even laughing at that myself, a bit stern, umm, so honestly, he ruled his class with a rod of iron). When you were in his class YOU DID ART.........whether you were good at it or not. His teaching methods may not have been the most politically correct, and often left a lot to be desired but his students used to turn out some fabulous works. I was in his class for the last three years of my school life, and despite his teaching manner, I learned an awful lot from him, and as art to me was like cat nip to a cat, I got along fine, even gaining an A in my exams! I must have done something right, although you could never tell as this teacher never smiled. Remember that cop show from the 1970's called 'Jason King'? That's the one with the actor Peter Wyngarde who played the title role, well this teacher was the spitting image of him, hair, mustache, dress sense, but with less smiling.

So with a full blown top of the range stage area, great art department, what more could this school have to offer? A fifth form common room that's what.

Of course, being 11, this room was out of bounds, but ooooh it was so intoxicating. As the tour led us all up the steps to the second floor of the concourse, we entered the science department. Walking down the long corridor we peered wide eyed and open mouthed inside the various classes on either side of us. These rooms were actual laboratories, there was such excitement in the air, as we innocently dreamed of curing the common cold by the end of the school term or inventing an invisible rocket......there is no limit when you're that age, anything seems possible.

At the end of the corridor we passed through some double doors and the smell of coffee hit us.

"Oh and that's the 5th form common room" announced our tour guide teacher.

We all 'oowed' in amazement, not at the coffee, but at the 'grown up' area.

"Of course you're not allowed in there" she continued.

And the 'oow's' quickly turned into 'Uuuhhhh's'.

But as the teacher announced this, a good looking blonde boy of about 8 foot 3........(he was probably 6 foot).........walked out of the common room (in slow motion!) dressed in jeans, t-shirt, with a guitar over his back. I drifted into little girl heaven.

WOW.......'this is the coolest room' were my thoughts.

As the door very slowly closed behind him I could see a group of pretty girls who actually looked like models sitting on a leather sofa surrounded by handsome boys, they were chatting and laughing and didn't look like they were in a school at all. I also noticed a small bar (an actual bar! Where they served coffee of course....the school wasn't 'that' liberal). Music was playing inside and posters of the likes of The Sweet, Hendrix, Deep Purple covered the walls. This room didn't appear to have windows so the lighting was low and moody, could this room get any better. Looking down at my school uniform of black skirt, red jumper and biscuit coloured shirt, I also realized all the students in that room were in casual clothes, like real people!

From then on, whenever I had reason to be in the area of the science department and I had to pass the common room doors it would always have this magical effect on me..........the land of the unknown which held strangely alluring and exciting possibilities. It also probably didn't happen like this but it seemed each time we did walk by that room 'What Becomes of the Broken Hearted' was being played inside, and without fail it would send my 'older than her years' friend Sharon into unnecessary tears over, 'Gaz' or 'Baz' or 'Daz'.....or whatever the name was of that particular months boyfriend.

By the time I reached 15 and was allowed in the common room my excitement was very short lived.

Do you know what? It was just a room with no window's, low lighting, sofas, posters on the wall and coffee.........I mean, what's thrilling about that?...........'huff'.

So that first year of secondary school crikey, it was, as you might gather, exciting, interesting, confusing, stressful, fabulous, all wound up into one. I'd been at the school about 7 or 8 months, and in the school classroom one day and we were half way through a history lesson. The teacher was actually one of the better ones. Other class mates would go green with envy when they heard you had Mr.Arkel as your history teacher as he had a nice way of making the beheading of historical types rather funky, interesting and entertaining.

During this lesson he was curious to know if we'd been listening to him a few weeks previous when he taught us the different religions and the implications they had in historical times.

"Right, can anyone give me examples of faiths, I'll start you off, Catholic" he said, commanding the room.

Someone put their hand up "Is Roman Catholic one sir" asked one of the lads.

"Yes, that's correct, anymore"? He asked.

"Jewish" said another boy, although I remember after this a lot of the class giggled as it came out "JEeewiisH" due to the poor boys voice breaking.

I'd recently heard something on the news with regards to religion so up went my hand, "Sir, Sir" I said all excited.

"Yes Shelley" he said "what have you come up with"?

"Prostitutes Sir", I confidently announced.

"Er" he looked down at the floor and turned around to face the wall then he turned back and smiled,

"I think you mean Protestant, prostitute is something completely different".

"Oh, so what's that sir?" one of the class asked in all innocence.

"I think you should ask your parents that one when you get home" he said.

There was no giggling and sniggling in the class we were all as clueless as each other, very innocent times.

End of the school day and I went home, Mum was out the back tending the garden, and my Dad was in the sitting room. I planted myself on the rug in between the TV and him.

"Dad" I said "can I ask you something"?
"Arrrr go on then, what"? He said.
I looked directly at him, "What's a prostitute"?........and I sat and waited eagerly for my reply.
"WHERE HAVE YA....WHY....I MEAN WHO....WHAT DO YOU WANT TO KNOW THAT FOR?" He seemed shocked and became very panicky standing up and looking out of the window waving erratically desperately trying to get my Mum's attention.
So I explained the best way I could about the afternoon's history lesson.
"Ohhhh, Oh I see" he said sitting down. "Well"....He continued...."it's, er, it's, it's a very naughty lady" he said rubbing his face.
"Oh, why don't they just call a naughty lady and naughty lady then"? I quizzed.
"Owww I don't know, sometimes they just don't" he said all frazzled, "now go on, go and make ya Dad a cuppa tea", then as I walked away he muttered under his breath "ya do ask me some things".

Five to six weeks later Mum and a couple of her friends had gathered jumble together to do a sale in aid of raising funds for my school to take a class of children (a class that I belonged to obviously) to The Playhouse in Nottingham to see the play 'The Widowing Of Mrs Holroyd'.
Living two doors away and due to the fact their garden was mainly grass with flower beds down the sides the jumble sale was held in Mabel Bent's garden. Her husband Bill....Bill Bent (you can't make these fabulous names up) had set up all these foldable tables in their garden to house the various jumble, clothes, kitchen wear, children's toys, etc. Mabel and Bill we're a lovely

couple and their daughter Gwen was really nice too, very kind I remember.

Gwen would sometimes look after me if Mum and Dad had a night out and we would spend the evenings all very girlie, she would glam me up in make-up and jewellery, and then I'd do a one woman show to a one woman audience. It was very exciting for a kid. Looking back, not that she needed to be, but she was always on a diet and would enter our house with a bag full of make-up, jewels, sparkly nice things, and bottles of PLJ. This was the most disgusting drink I ever did taste, it was so bitter. I think the aim of the product was to get 'slimmers' away from the sweet cravings they may have by trying to retrain their taste to appreciate sour. Yuk, it was awful. As for tasting the stuff it's my own fault, I pestered Gwen until she gave me a little sip one evening.

From a very young age I would go to 'The Bents' house two doors down and put on shows for them, singing, dancing, magic, impressions (mainly of other neighbours) that was always met with appreciative applause and laughter. My Mum and Mabel were pals and my Dad (Tony) and Bill would often nip for a pint together. I don't know how things are today, but back then most adults where I lived as a child were pretend Aunts and Uncles.

Meanwhile back to sale day, with the jumble now set out Gwen began to let in the customers at the gate, and there were a lot. I was on duty at the bric-a-brac table with Mabel, my Mum was on the cake stall and my Dad was just milling about chatting to people, whilst various neighbour type ladies looked after the other tables.

The sun was out and so were the crowds, the garden was full of people. It was going great, the stock was getting lower as people picked up their bargains, so after a few hours Mabel told me to,

"Go and get a cake from ya Mum duckie, have a little break".
I wandered over to Mum, she passed me a cake whilst chatting to
a lady and her husband and I then wandered about the busy
tables nibbling on the fairy cake. There was one woman customer,
who to me, seemed to be acting a little odd, so I casually
wandered around the garden watching her. I figured soon after
this exactly why she was acting odd. She was stealing. I looked
on as she, in the busy hive of activity in the garden picked up a
china figurine, looked at it and then put it in her pocket and
wandered to the next stall. I wasn't sure what to do? I'd never
been witness to anything like that before, and in all honesty I
found it a little upsetting. I couldn't make up my mind what to do,
I mean, would 'I' get into trouble for tell-tailing on an adult? I
decided the best option for now would be to keep an eye on her
so I continued to follow her. She carried on by 'lifting' a small
toy, various bits and pieces of children's clothing, a couple of
items of junk jewellery and last but not least three men's ties.
'Could it be possible this lady would get to the last table and then
pay for 'all' the things' I thought. But she didn't. Quite sharp'ish
she made a bee-line for the gate. Well, I'm sorry but I couldn't
let that happen and I needed to tell my Dad, so I jumped up onto
a chair that was sitting at the side of a stall and at the top of my
voice shouted over to my Dad who was in a clump of chatting
men, "DAD, DAD, THE LADY IN THE BLUE TOP THERE
(pointing) STOP HER, SHE'S A PROSTITUTE".
It went very quiet................and everyone just stopped in their
tracks.
I suddenly saw my Mum's face as she pushed through the crowd
"Shelley, why on earth have you said that"?
"Because she's taking lots of things without paying" I said, and as
this was happening the woman tried to rush off but Mabel and
Gwen managed to stop her and asked to see in her pockets and

bag. There were raised voices but sure enough on examination of her bag even more items than I'd seen her take were discovered. Honestly a jumble sale, some people. And believe it or not a couple of years after this I was at my Aunties jumble sale where a similar thing happened, what is wrong with people.

Mabel was having none of it and so phoned the police.

Once the kafuffle had ended and the jumble sale had come to a close, with customers, thieves and police all gone we sat in a circle around a table shaded by a pretty parasol with the ladies counting the day's takings and the men chatting about creosote or something equally as boring and I was on my second fairy cake. Not only had enough money been raised for my class to go the theatre there was enough over to donate towards future trips for the school.

The ladies sat there sipping tea and chatting.

"Shelley ma'duck" said Mabel, "What made you call that lady, ya know, the lady who stole the things, a prostitute duckie" she asked whilst putting her hand over her mouth to cover her smiles.

My Mum piped up "Ohhhh yes young lady, I'd like to know that as well".

So I sat and told them about school, the history lesson, my Dad, and then my thoughts about the day's events and how I thought the lady had been naughty.

Nothing much happened after that, except for Mabel and Gwen laughing and my Mum putting her cup of tea down, standing up from the table and shouting ……….

"T-O-N-Y"!

My friend Susan had told me about an open audition for a show at the Theatre Royal in Nottingham. She insisted, "You should go for that, they want singers that can dance, and dancers that can sing". It covered all areas.

In an attempt at the moral support club we both decided to go down to Hoofers Dance Studios in the centre of the city on the Monday morning for the auditions. I was 18 and she was 20, so we were placed in slightly different age groups, she went in first, and I sat waiting with the many other hopefuls in the corridor. We all began the day looking bright eyed and bushy tailed, but the morning soon became lunch time and then we were into the afternoon. We could all hear the piano from the rehearsal studio the other side of the door, and instructions from a director and then every now and again the voice of a choreographer. Every so often the door would open and little sad faces would exit, until each group had been whittled down to six.

After quite some time Susan emerged looking like a sweaty, crumpled version of herself not to mention a little disappointed. "I haven't got in" she said "But ya know I kinda expected that, I was fine with the songs but I'm not the best dancer and I just couldn't keep up with the what 'they' referred to as basic routines" she said.

"Oh never mind Sue" I said, are you going to go now, or wait for me"? I inquired.

"Well I should go, I was in there for ages and I mean how long will you be? No, no, I'd better go, I have a dentist appointment at half past and I don't want to be late, didn't realize it would take this long". We arranged a meet the following day then off she went.

The group of girls I'd been placed with were called into the dance studio soon after this. There were sixteen of us. We'd stretched and limbered up so much I'm sure we were all 3 inches taller than when we arrived.

"OK everyone", called a chap with glasses hanging around his neck on a chain, if you could all get around the piano" (although he referred to it as a pi-aarr-no) "We need to do some scales before we sing the song". What's all this 'we' I thought, as I watched the bearded gent downing his tea.

Anyhow that's what happened. With four faces looking at us from the other side of a long table, we sang.

La la la la la la la la la lahhhh..........We did this several times, and various other warm up techniques and then the song. "What is it that we're living for, applause, applause" and so on.

This went on for some time being broken up into groups of four, then twos, then solos.

Eventually the be'speckled, but everso flamboyant chap walked over, "You, you, you, you you (he said pointing) you, you, you, you and you stay, the rest of you can go, thank you very much", he said with a forced smile and did a swift about turn heading towards the table and then writing notes. All this sounds very cold doesn't it, and to a degree it is very cold, auditions can be brutal.

I once went all the way to London from Nottingham only to be told at the check in desk for the auditions "No, sorry Shelley you're not what we're looking for".....so I went back home within an hour and ate my own body weight in chocolate on the train. Affect me, who me? nah, not that you'd notice.

So out of our sixteen, ten were left, of which I was one and we knew that ten had to be shaved to six.

"Ladies if you'd like to go and warm up just while we have a short break and discuss a few things, then we'll call you back for the dance routines" said a tall pale lady.

We were then sent back out into the corridor, where a woman with a tray of hot coffee and sandwiches passed us going back into the studio.

I sat on the floor and attempted to touch my toes whilst watching the other girls.......all putting on their 'tap' shoes.

Er.....Tap shoes? I looked at the girl at the side of me.

"Tap shoes"? I said.

"Yes, it was in the memo they sent out, didn't you get one, did no one phone you"? She said looking all leggy, blonde and knowledgeable.

Not wanting to look like a right numpty, I just said "Ohhh, yeh, yeh, it just totally slipped my mind, been soooo busy".

But it hadn't, and the everso s-l-i-g-h-t problem was even if I had've had any information previously, I hadn't a pair of tap shoes anyhow. This was due to the fact I didn't do tap.

It was there and then I should have just owned up and said with arms stretched out wide........"HELLO EVERYONE, NOW HEAR THIS....I HAVE NO TAP SHOES, I HAVE NEVER DONE TAP, I PROBABLY WILL NEVER DO TAP AND SO NOW I SHALL BE RETURNING HOME, GOODNIGHT AND THANKYOU".

But noooooo, I decided to go with the far more stupid option of finding the girls that had already been in auditioning, of which most were still congregating in the coffee bar area and asking "Er hello, sorry, er, could I ask, do any of you have a pair of tap shoes size 6 umm? I've accidentally forgotten mine".

Yes I'd accidentally forgotten to even buy a pair. Why do we do these things to ourselves instead of just owning up?

As it happens, yes a kind soul (or should that be a kind sole!) did have a pair, size 6, so after putting them on I tip tapped my way back down the corridor. Clip clop, clip clop.

All the girls were confidently shuffle-stepping over every inch of the corridor and I just sat there looking down at the black shiny shoes.

'I hope these are magic shoe's' I thought 'cos that's the only way I'm going to get through this audition now'.

It wasn't long before we were being beckoned back into the large mirrored dance studio. Yes, I could actually watch myself going wrong.

The beautifully slim choreographer dressed from head to toe in black sprang into action and danced her way through the five minute routine, backed by the pianist who was able to play and watch the lady as she effortlessly tapped, swayed and glided herself around the floor. A few of the girls tried to imitate her movements on the spot, making the rest of us feel very inadequate.

The tall slim lady (who resembled a 'Biba' poster) finished the routine by brushing her very long grey silky hair to one side and hardly breaking a sweat with hands on hips said "OK ladies, so just follow me, let's see what you've got".

I actually had nothing, apart from the biggest knot in my stomach, but decided to give it a go, I could hardly just stand there could I. Besides I'd come this far after all and oddly enough I didn't look half as nervous as the girl at the side of me. The piano started, and the choreographer shouted instructions at us.

"Shuffle and step and turn turn turn, and step and tap, and tap and shuffle and clap and………." There was so much to remember, and I thought patting your head and rubbing your tummy was hard, but hey I wasn't the only one struggling to remember all the instructions, and the nervous girl to the side of me after a tense 30 minutes of rat-a-tat-tapping chaos just burst into tears and fled from the room.

We all just stood and watched in silence as a lady who been sitting in on the audition at the table, gently stood up and followed the distressed girl out into the corridor, hopefully with a little cup of human kindness.

It wasn't long before the choreographer was calling the dance moves out to us all once again, but with a man down we were now even more exposed.

".....and turn and turn and shuffle, and............" I knew the moves I just wasn't sure where all the tappy bits were s'posed to come in. So I looked at the choreographer's feet. They didn't really match her face and body. In that while 'they' were of fine attractive bone structure and toned body, her feet looked like she'd put them through a cheese grater. They had all the signs that they'd worked for many a year, with scars, lumps and bumps. I tried to concentrate. My theory was as I was quite a good mimic (which didn't impress 'some' of my neighbours) that's what I'll do, mimic the taps and steps.

'Oh I see, when she steps there that's where the tap shuffle happens'.

It was microwave learning, as in a lot of information in a short space of time.

I looked straight ahead. From the reflection in the mirror I could see everyone in the group looking very determined with straight serious faces.

'Oh in for a penny, its doubtful I'm going to get in anyhow' I thought, so with the next batch of instructions I decided to just enjoy myself during the routine and smiled, and smile I did, to the point where I looked like I'd woken up with a coat hanger in my mouth. Shuffle, tap, shuffle, tap, tap, tap. I started to quite enjoy it, and even though I went wrong a few times, quite a few times actually, OK, ok, you've dragged it out of me, I did a few correct steps, I also managed a few 'Woo's' as the dance went on.

This routine was repeated and repeated, which I didn't actually need to write the second repeat, if you see my meaning.
After quite some time of doing this and other little routines we were all on the verge of collapse but the choreographer called "One more time", standing there looking like a glowing mermaid.
We did 'the' routine again with a final burst of energy.
The piano stopped and we all fell to the floor. My little toes were throbbing. Not only had I subjected them to a completely new dance style but also, alien shoes. I peeled the shoes off and rubbed my toes, 'ouch that hurts, but heck it felt good'.

The director stood from his chair and as the choreographer walked over to him the two of them, together with the other two adjudicators in the room chatted in a circle with hushed voices.
We, the 'Auditionette's' (that's a 1940's vocal group I'm thinking of putting together) just panted our breath back sitting on the floor.
Finally after a while the director spoke.
"Thank you for your efforts today" (efforts! Cheek)
"Unfortunately we can't use all of you, but those of you we don't use we will be keeping your name on file. So here are the names we'd like to see on the 21st to start rehearsals". He then reeled off 6 names, the last one being MINE! Your shocked aren't you, but I'm guessing not half as shocked as I was.

I promptly sent myself to the dance shop the following day and purchased my own tap shoes. The rehearsals for me were v-e-r-y hard work, and even when there was a break I'd find a quiet corner to keep going over the steps.
On the opening night of the show after the first of two tap numbers I noticed the choreographer floating in the wings with

encouraging smiles and gestures. As we ran off stage I quickly said "can I speak to you after the show"?

"Of course dear" she replied.

So after the show I tracked her down to the Green Room where she stood looking very elegant. Dressed in the most silky and clingy of dresses, so much so it looked like it had been sprayed on her, she stood with a long slim cigarette in one hand and glass of wine in the other and as I walked up to her I said,

"I have a confession to make, please don't be angry, but here goes, before the audition I'd never put on a pair of tap shoes, let alone actually done any tap. I've kind of picked up where I should be tapping throughout the rehearsal period".

She stood for a moment just looking at me. Eventually she put her wine down on the table and then said to me,

"We-ll, oh my, I didn't really notice in all honesty as you've always shown enthusiasm, if not a little clumsy, in rehearsals I know you've struggled I put it down to nerves and during the auditions I have a confession to make myself, I didn't really notice your feet. You were smiling so much, that's what drew me towards you".

So those sleepless nights were a waste of time then.

What I need to mention is the same day as the audition on returning home I poured out the day's dramas to my Mum and she casually as you like said "Oh yeh, I meant to tell you that a letter came for you yesterday, ya Dad put it on the shelf. Didn't you see it"?

No.......no I didn't.

Would I have gone to the audition with the knowledge of the expected tap routine though? I'm thinking probably not.

Picture the scene, early 1980's, Nottingham. That sounds like I'm setting up a 1950's American detective show........'she walked into the room, I could tell this wasn't going to go well as she'd forgotten her dance shoes'.........let's not start that again.

I was rehearsing for the musical show 'My Fair Lady' at the Nottingham Arts Theatre. Although we, the cast that is, used to call it, 'My Furry Ludo', it amused us, and was possibly infused with Barley Wine one late rehearsal night.
It was a Friday and I'd spent the day in town meeting up with a friend having lunch and a general plod around the shops.
Before rehearsals I'd decided to have a lesson at the Patricia James (no relation) School Of Dance. I had lessons each week with Pat, but I would try to cram in some extra lessons here and there if I could when rehearsals were on. Just a way of trying to keep my mind and body balanced when doing the kind of shows where you needed to be on top form.
Before my lesson approached I had a spare half an hour so decided to nip just over the main road into 'Boots' and spend money I didn't have.
I'd only been in the shop browsing for around 5 minutes when I spotted my sister-in-law, Trish. Well, Pat as she's known to most, Patricia James (yes, relation), but not 'that' Patricia James (also, not related to each other).
I called out "Trish"................."Trish"................."Trish", but she couldn't have heard me as she carried on walking by. So I decided to have a bit of fun, I proceeded to follow her and her thick flowing shoulder length hair around the shop doing silly voices each time I caught up with her.
What? Really?. You're questioning 'that' after we'd renamed the show 'My Furry Ludo'.

So my trail of comedy torture (for her) played out like this...........she stopped at the hair shampoo and conditioners, and I peered over the shampoo stocked shelves by saying in a very cartoon style voice "HELLO YOUNG LADY, WELL FANCYyyyyyy SEEING YOU HERE"....

She carried on ignoring me and walked down the next aisle.

'Oh right, that's how we're going to do this is it' I thought. So I followed her to the next section. As she stood looking at the list of ingredients on a product I peeped around the corner of the shelving display stating in a voice similar to Kenneth Williams, "WELL I DON'T BELIEVE IT, THERE SHE IS, OWWW THERE SHE IS, WHAT'S SHE UP TO I WONDER".

I couldn't understand it she never even glanced my way. Oh I see what she's doing, so I carried on with 'my' doings.

She reached the make up counter.

"NOW THEN DUCK, BE CAREFUL, WE DON'T WANT YA LOOKING LIKE CO CO THE CLOWN NOW DO WE" I growled with all the charm of Louis Armstrong.

She never batted an eyelid, even though she did seem to be 'shifting' quicker around the store at this point.

I'd now got the giggles, well, it was fun (I think, yes it was) and I knew she would also find it funny, even though she wasn't showing it..............yet.

She stopped at the toothpastes. Right 'time to do the suave, seductive voice' I thought.

"OH I SAY, ONE HAS TO GET THEIR TOOTHYPEGS NICE AND CLEAN UM UM UM DOSENT ONE, BRUSHY BRUSHY BRUSHY".

Nope, still she refused to join in with my jollities and headed for the cash out. I'd been following her around the shop just over 10 minutes and it had become one of those things that due to her non response just became increasingly funnier.

'Oh we'll get to the cash out and she will turn and say "You're off ya head you are" and we'd laugh about it'.........Perhaps?

A gent was being served and 'Trish' was next in the queue, so I stood behind her, and when I say behind her, I was soooo close behind her that my nose was almost touching her hair, it was then I gave my final warped speech.

In a very nasally fashion I said,

"WELL, HELLO THERE PRETTY LADDDYYYYYYY, ITS ME, ME, OWW ELLO, ELLO, CHEEKY, OWW ELLO, ELLO, WHO'S A LOVELY GIRL THEN, YOU ARE, YOU ARE, WHO'S A CHEEKY GIRL, YOU ARE, YOU ARE, BOO-BOO-BOO-BOO-BOO".

'Trish' then put her full basket of purchases on the floor and ran out of the shop, much to the surprise of the man being served the cashier, and even me.

"Oww, I wonder what's wrong with her"? Said the shop assistant. The man shook his head puzzled, and I said,

"I don't know, but the funny thi……………….." And as the words came out of my mouth, I felt this heavy weight hit my stomach like a stone boulder.

OH NO…………IT WASN'T TRISH! or indeed 'any' Patricia James. I'd suddenly realized that it was only a few days previous I'd seen my Mum and she'd mentioned that Trish had had her hair cut really short. I 'was' paying attention-ish, ok, so I was singing along to the radio at the same time, Oops a daisy.

We, as in male customer, cashier and I looked at each other. I found myself saying,

"Er, I don't know, there are some funny people about".

Well I should know. I was one of them.

In an obscure feeling of guilt that the shop had lost out on quite a substantial sale I found myself going into the disowned basket on the floor and taking out some shampoo and toothpaste to which I announced rather sheepishly,

"Erm, and I might as well take these as well please".

I wonder if Trish's double ever told anyone about being followed around 'Boots' by this crazy woman....crazier still.........were you that doppel-ganger?

Has not receiving the correct information or not even getting informed ever helped or hindered you?

Favourite overheard quote of the time.

"...well I've made it nicer now, I've bought a little lamp and some cushions, before that it was just a little room with flies in."

Chapter Six… Love Me Love My Dog

If you don't treat a pet like part of the family, then in my opinion
you shouldn't really own a pet. All through my life pets have
played an important role and in many ways dictated the life style
I've had, especially growing up. A pet is a member of the family,
simple.
Border Collies were always a draw to my family, such beautiful
dogs, and so intelligent. So after losing our beloved Trixie and my
Dad stating,
"That's it, we are 'never' having a dog again" (due to the total
excruciating upset it caused the family in losing her) I figured,
well, that's that.
So around a year later we were traveling by the RSPCA animal
shelter in Radcliff on Trent, Nottinghamshire and it came as
somewhat of a surprise when my Dad did an about turn with the
car.
"What's happening" asked Mum.
"Goin' to see if they've got any German Shepherds" replied Dad.
"Are we now" said Mum, and you just knew by her tone, there was
no way we were going to return home with an Alsatian. Not for
any other reason other than Mum was a little bit nervous of
them. She'd been nipped by one as a child and it had made her
slighter wary of them. In her words "they are lovely dogs, lovely
faces and of course I'd never see one hurt". However, she felt to
own one was a big responsibility.
Anyhow, we arrived and went in and I think I spent the next hour
crying! I was 17 my hormones were on overdrive, add that to the
fact I love animals and seeing all these precious creatures just
wanting a loving home……..I was in bits.
My Dad spied an Alsatian,

"Oh 'ay's a beauty in't he" he said to my Mum who was practically 'in' a pen with a little Jack Russell dog due to her having backed off so much. The Alsatian did protest at being in his pen and barked and barked and barked.

"He is Tony, but he's everso noisy", said Mum.

"You would be if ya 'ad to stay in 'ere" said Dad backing up the dogs frustrated barks.

This scruffy bloke walked by us and my Mum asked,

"S'cuse me duckie do you have any Border Collies"?

"Nah" came back the reply "No sooner gerrem in, people 'aye 'em" said the chap.

Oddly enough my Mum then proceeded to have a look around. Meanwhile, I was hunting for the Samaritans phone number……..Oh, those little faces, it was killing me.

All of a sudden my Mum called "Tony, here"……..and in a rather large pen with a Heinz 57 variety of dogs all shapes and sizes, way back in the corner all nervous and shivering was a thin border collie. Mum got hold of the scruffy chap,

"Oi, duckie, can I have a look at the dog over there in the corner, the collie".

"Oh, didn't know we 'ad any in" he said with all the interest of a wet flannel. He climbed into the pen and picked up the little black and white dog by the scruff of her neck and passed 'it' over the fencing to my Mum.

"Ow come here duckie" said Mum as she got hold of the little under fed cutie. It was like a match made in heaven. Mum cuddled dog, and dog snuggled Mum. "Oh Tony, we can't leave her, we've got to take her home" she said within two minutes of their cuddles.

"How do ya know it 'is' a 'her'"? He asked.

"I just do" she said. Sure enough on closer inspection she was right, the dog was indeed female.

"Ow Tony, Tony! I can't leave her" said Mum gripping hold of the dog and being very close to tears.

"Arrrhhhh alright then, we'll 'ave her then my duck, don't be gerrin' ya sen all upset", said Dad, he hadn't really needed much persuasion......it was a dog after all.

It was at that instant the dog became part of our family, and what a gorgeous dog she was too.

After some chat in an office and then signing the adoption forms at the centre a woman who worked there looked over the reception counter at our little mutt and said "so you're adopting Lady are you".

My Mum looked at her and said,

"Who? Oh I see, well she might be Lady to you, but this is the new addition to our family, and her name is Muffin".

My Dad and I looked surprised at each other, it was almost as if Mum had planned to go to the animal shelter all along and brain washed my Dad into stopping the car there!

We discovered from the receptionist that 'Lady' was approximately six months old, and had been found and brought in by a truck driver. He spotted her on the hard shoulder of the M1, terrified. Grrrrrrrrr, (blood boiling time) why would someone do that? Why? And thank goodness for the likes of the truck driver.

A month followed and a woman from the re-homing centre came to our house to check on 'Muffin'.

"I see she's settled in" said the lady laughing as Muffin lay upside down very casually on the sofa.

That little dog soon became part of our extended family too, and an invite for tea or the like would be instantly followed with "oh and bring Muffin". She certainly was popular, just like in the past with Trixie, wherever we went so did Muffin, a very well behaved house trained doggie.

There now follows a name drop alert. Working with Danny LaRue in the 1990's, and on his arrival at the venue said to me "It's alright if I bring my dog in isn't it", to which I excitedly replied "alright, it's practically the law as far as I'm concerned". From then on his bookings would always include his 'fur baby'. As he said to me when explaining about turning down a contract due to the theatre not allowing him to take his dog...."No doggie, no Danny".

Our beautiful dog settled in relatively fast, she had such a lovely character, and our neighbours warmed to her quite quickly too. So it would've been 8 months or so later after getting 'Muffin' that my Dad met a chap through my Uncle Geoff. He'd introduced my Dad to said bloke at the Oakleigh Lodge Social Club, a local venue where on numerous occasions I would sing, not just for the sake of it! I'd actually been booked.
For arguments sake let's call the chap 'Gary'. Now Gary fancied himself as a bit of an impresario. My Dad had been selling me saying how I was venturing out into the big wide world of showbiz and if he knew anywhere that needed a singer to let him know. Well 'Gary' took this information a stage further and for some unknown reason took it upon himself to act as my agent for a while. I didn't like it............because I didn't like him. He was quite an arrogant man and spoke down to me like he'd been in the business all of his life, when actually he knew nothing about 'show', he was a builder, and owned a small building company! My Mum wasn't keen either. She referred to him when in conversation with my Dad as 'a patronising little squirt'. He was a little short stocky fella who would swagger about in his sheepskin coat and have sunglasses on indoors and puff away on the end of a cigar, all very Arthur Daley. We'd known him three months

before we knew the name of his wife, Glenda, all we knew her as before then was 'the little woman'. He really was a joy to know! Although I was already working here and there, he got me five gigs in various venues, and insisted on being at all but one when I was booked to sing. I remember at the second gig I was singing a ballad and all I could hear was him 'BLA BLA BLA'ING' at the bar, being hushed by the audience around him..............'he' that had got me the booking, ironic. I wasn't impressed by him at all and I was desperate to find a way to ditch him without offending my Dad. I said this to my Mum and she said,

"It'll be alright duckie, he strikes me as the type that will get bored soon", so the situation carried on.

At the third booking, he didn't attend, had some building drama to sort out or something. The manager of the club paid me and I was shocked! He gave me three times the amount that 'Gary' had been passing over at the end of a night. My Dad hit the roof. At the fourth gig a week later my Dad told him to basically 'stuff any future bookings where the sun don't shine' (I've seriously cleaned that up). My Mum quite rightly had seen through him early on and said how she thought he was 'dodgy'. The day before the last of the five gigs Mum had a phone call from Glenda, she pleaded with Mum to "come to the house and have tea with us to 'get all this upset sorted out' after the show". Mum said she sounded like a nice woman and so decided it wouldn't hurt to go along and at least meet her, maybe 'Gary' would be different in his home surroundings and we'd see a nicer side to him (don't hold your breath dear reader!). We later found out that Glenda had been primed by her husband to make the phone request.

The gig was an afternoon affair at a private garden party up on Mapperley Plains in Nottingham. Wow! Talk about how the other half live. The nice couple holding the party owned several dogs and when I asked would it be ok for Mum and Dad to come along, the conversation got around to "are they ok with dogs" and one thing led to another, so they told me "yes of course bring your dog". Muffin had a fabulous afternoon, spoilt with various tit-bits, dog treats and numerous people adoring her, so she had a fabulous time and played in the garden with the dogs that lived at the house. It was a lovely day actually, singing in the sunshine, you can't beat it.

We even got to meet Glenda, and what a glamour puss she was. She was nice, quietly spoken, and quite a delicate lady. After 5pm it was time for us to leave and let the party revelers carry on, so we ventured not too far down the lane to the home of 'Gary' and Glenda.

"Ow eh", said my Mum as we drew up to the gate "Tony, look, it's one of them houses where you drive in one side and drive out the other", (she of course meant the driveway.....the house wasn't a drive thru'!....) "flippin' eck, ow eh they've got some money".

And she was right, they did have some money. Woo, t'was rather ostentatious.......that's an exciting word isn't it.......'woo'.

But hey, if you've got it flaunt it I guess. The biggest private house I'd ever been in at that time for sure. The hallway alone housed a grand piano.

"Ohhhh how lovely, who plays piano"? Mum asked enthusiastically.

"No one" said 'Gary', "I just saw it and wanted it" he bragged.

I'd also felt the same way about David Cassidy since I was ten! The hallway floor shone so clearly like a mirror, I'm sure no one had walked on it before us as it didn't have one mark on it, not one.

"Alright if we bring the dog in" Dad asked "she's no trouble, but I'm not leaving her in the car in this heat".

Glenda said, "Ohhh I should think that'll be alright, er, wont it 'Gary', er, I'm sure it will, she's no trouble yeh"?

And we all stood and looked at the master of the house as he left us waiting like he was going to announce the winner of a talent show...

"Arrhh alright" he said through gritted teeth.

Off my Dad went and minutes later was back with the dog. With her waggy tail in fifth gear she sniffed here and she sniffed there, and before we knew it we were all being guided into the sitting room.

"Ohhhhh Glenda" said my Mum "what a beautiful room duckie". It really was...... I'd never seen a room like it, before or since actually, it was a little bit like walking onto a Hollywood film set. It was huge. White walls, floor to ceiling windows, which was quite unusual back then. Two cream sofas big enough to fit a football team on, and two mahoosive arm chairs. There was a huge cabinet in the corner that cleverly hid a T.V., and there were little glass and chrome scatter tables here and there, and two enormous plants that look like they had come directly from the 'Day of the Triffids' set which perched proudly either side of the double glass doors and a large plush cream sheepskin rug that sat in the middle of the room as centre piece (possibly to go with 'Gary's' sheepskin coat). Glenda made tea and the pretty china tea cups rattled sweetly as she came back into the room with a tray full of tea hospitality. Meanwhile the Lord of the Manor, who'd opted for whiskey instead of tea, had been telling us how he started with nothing, and owed nothing, and if someone doesn't do the job right for him from the off, then they are out, no excuses and no time wasters. In his words "no time for sentimentality and all that 'bleep' rubbish" he declared.

As glam Glenda passed the tea round 'Gary' moaned she should have made some snacks for when they returned, she 'knew' after all they were going to have company. She didn't answer back. He then snapped at her soon after this as there was a smudge mark on one of the glass doors, as he said he "didn't marry her and provide so that she could sit on her ar*e all day". This man really was a delight.

My Mum, trying to detract from the uncomfortable situation said how Glenda had got the place beautiful, so Glenda offered to take Mum on a tour of the house, which Mum happily accepted. While this was happening 'Gary' lectured to my Dad and I about how 'I' needed to 'broaden my horizons' and with his help it could happen, 'the money thing had just been a misunderstanding'.................umm had it.

No sooner had Mum and Glenda returned to the sitting room after the tour of the house 'Gary' started on her again,

"Do we have to die of thirst before you get us more drinks" he snapped. Obviously the charm school was closed the day he went. On and on and on he whined, Glenda not answering back once. My Dad butted in at one point saying,

"Oh come on 'Gary' gee it a rest now pal".

But good ole' 'Gary' was now the other side of 3 large scotches and there was no stopping him. At one point we could just see this cloud of cigar smoke with niggling noises coming out of it! Poor Glenda looked so embarrassed. After a while my Dad announced how we really should be going.....when 'Gary' spoke over him with the statement,

"NOBODY is goin' nowhere, here we are having a nice drink (well he was) and 'SHE' (looking over at Glenda) isn't going to spoilt it for everyone else".

I wasn't quite sure what Glenda had done exactly to deserve that, but while I was thinking these thoughts 'Gary' staggered over to the hi-fi system insisting we hear 'this'...........whatever it was......we never heard it you see, as it was then a strange chain of events began.

Firstly Glenda started to cry, and I mean sob. So my Mum tried her best to comfort her. My Dad then suggested to 'Gary' that he should maybe 'calm down a bit', with 'Gary' insisting "I AM CALM" (in a very loud and un-calm fashion). I had the dog's lead in my hand and gently called "Muffin, come here", thinking 'well, if I get the dog on the lead we'll be that bit more organized to leaving this glamorous hell hole'. Muffin who'd been laying near Dad, got up, had a shake, started walking towards me, stopped, looked at 'Gary', walked towards the sheepskin rug, got right in the middle of it, squat herself down

and...

....
....had a poo!....................................
....
....

..............Yes, our faces were like that too.

We all looked on in total shock as the sweet little Border Collie finished her 'doings' had a good shake, wagged her tail and trotted back to Dad.

"OHHHHH GLENDA", Mum cried............"I am so very, so very sorry, oh I don't know what to say, Ohhhhhhh Glenda".................
and then there was quiet again and we all just looked at the 'gift' sitting in the middle of the rug. 'Gary' not uttering a word knocked back the rest of his drink in one, and my Dad came out with the statement of all statements.

"Well................'owze never done that before", almost as if they should feel privileged the dog had done it at their house but never anywhere else.

Towards the end of this sweeping statement I saw my Mum go into her handbag and get out a pack of paper hankies and then crawl onto the rug picking up the.........well, you know what.

Mum must have said sorry a dozen times whist doing this. Glenda looked nervously at her husband who filled his glass again and then stood glaring out of the window.

"Right then" my Dad said "I think that's us leavin' then".......and we did, I'd got the dog on the lead. Dad had the car keys in his hand, and my Mum had........well, you know what.

Glenda showed us out, but not before kindly pointing Mum towards the dustbin area, saying in a hushed tone,

"Please don't worry you can pop the poop in there".

We heard the door quietly close behind us and as Mum deposited the 'doings' into the bin she said,

"Oww I say Tony, they've even got shiny dustbins as well".

On the way home the car was full of laughter from yours truly and Dad, full of embarrassment from my Mum, and lots of fussy barking from the dog. Anyone else and I would have been ashamed our dog had done that, but 'Gary', let's just say, perfect. We never saw or heard anything from 'Gary' again. Strange that. Mum however did bump into Glenda in town a few months later around Christmas time and was surprised to hear that Glenda had often laughed to herself about Muffin and the sheep skin rug episode! Mum also learned that Glenda and 'Gary' had parted company a few weeks previous to the ladies meet. Glenda explained to Mum how she was wife number three and a fourth 'Mrs. Gary' was on the cards. Apparently this bloke was handy at giving out more than just criticism, and she'd had enough................so the dog must have sensed something in the house I'm assuming.

It was a couple of years before however around Christmas, you know that inbetweeny bit that sits with Christmas one side and New Year the other that we had another 'doggie doo time'! Total coincidence, but I'd just done a lunch time gig at the Oakleigh Lodge and some of Dad's side of the family had come to watch and then on Mum's request came to ours for tea afterwards. This time however 'doggie doo time' was down to pure excitement.

So there we all were, it was quite a houseful and basically everything seemed to happen at the same time. I remember my cousins Debbie and Pauline having a bit of a spat, and my Uncle Barrie shouting at them both to stop arguing. Mum had just come in the room with a trifle in a large dish, placed it on the table and Auntie had brought in the tea pot. Cousins still bickering, Uncle still shouting, Auntie poured the tea and all of a sudden one of the smoked glass tea-cups just randomly exploded, sending flying glass everywhere, mainly in the trifle. As this happened the dog climbed up onto the sofa, and then onto Uncle Barrie's back, where she very carefully balanced herself and proceeded to have a very long...wee.

At this point my Dad entered the room, there was a second or two of shock realization on his face as he stared at the chaos which consumed the sitting room, he then said,

"What the b****y 'ell's goin' on. Them two are arguing, the cups gone for a burton, trifles had it and the dog is p*****g down Barrie's back". It was a lot of information to take in.

Even though my Mum never did get over the Pyrex cups that let her down and ruined that perfect trifle, it wasn't all bad.

I'd never seen my Dad laugh so much that day. It certainly stopped the cousins from arguing as we all watched open mouthed as the dog continued to tiddle down uncles back..........the strange thing was, my uncle didn't move, he just sat there until she had finished, announcing as we were all in hysterics,

"Er, when ya'v quite finished all of ya, the dogs p*****g on me".

For two pins I'd have got her off him, but it was far too funny.

Oh, if only we'd have had mobile phones back then............£250 via 'You've Been Framed' for sure.

Talking of dogs tiddling (strange subject matter, I admit) ....I was doing a 1940's touring show, it was the late morning and as always we were there around 11am at the theatre to do our sound check for the afternoon matinee show. The whole cast plus band were on the stage and I noticed in the auditorium a beautiful dog, yes, a Border Collie. She was very friendly and as I did my own sound check she came up onto the stage and fussed around me, so I sang what I needed to sing and in the gaps had a little doggie cuddle fix. The lady she was with called from the lighting box,
"Is the dog bothering you"? And we all called out "no, she's fine". All but one of the shows cast that is. He didn't really make his feelings known either way, it was as if the dog wasn't there, he just ignored her. Most of our individual sound checks were taking around 5 minutes, just singing a little of each song and it was sorted. We all wanted to go and find somewhere to eat before the show so time was of the essence. Anyhow it came to 'his' sound check, the dog whisperer! Not. His sound check for no obvious reason to my ears, took forever. He went through every song in full. Already 15 minutes in and he still had several songs to go, the time was ticking by.
Well..... I swear, I thought I would never stop laughing. He was half way through his fifth song. The dog trots back up onto the stage, walked over to him, looked up at him as he's singing, and just decided to have a wee all over his foot. The rake of the stage at this particular theatre was quite a slope. He didn't look down once, just carried on singing, and the river of wee was trickling down from his foot to the edge of the stage.

It was already very, very funny, but the thing that was the cherry on the cake was the song he was singing....'Babbling Brook'............no joke.

The lovely thing about this whole story was the lady who owned the dog had been through quite a traumatic and terrible year, and had inherited the dog from a close family member............she said afterwards she never thought she would ever smile again, let alone laugh like that. Angels come in many disguises.

And what is it with these men that don't move and let the dog finish its duty! Respect? Fear? Just plain daft?....Lets 'paws' for thought on that one.

Ever owned a pet that has landed you in hot water?

Favourite overheard quote of the time.

".......oww you can't go from jumper to cotton in a day, why do you think dogs melt gradually!!!"

Chapter Seven... Right Said Fred

"Does this sound alright" I'd ask as I'd sing "yes sir, I can boogie, but I neeed-a-ceurtain song......."..........I'd be in the school yard with friend Karen. "I don't know? I'm trying to fill this in before English (she'd said writing in her essay book without looking at me) but stop singing it in their accent" would be her reply.
This has been an ongoing habit of mine all my life it's almost like accent tourettes. If I hear a strong accent I struggle not to imitate it, which is fine if it happens to be a song or something you've heard on the TV/radio. When it spills over into real life its embarrassing. I do love accents, and the diversity of so many on our small island it's amazing really. Sometimes when speaking to someone I've never met who holds a strong accent, I really have to check myself not to answer them back in their own accent. A friend of mine who teaches music once told me this is due to my brain hearing everything as a melody and hearing the accent as a tune. I love this romantic notion, and agree with it. But it brings very little comfort when you meet someone for the first time from Yorkshire and after they've said in a broad accent,
"'Ello luv, rayte nice ta meet ya, pity it's not sa warrm", you find yourself replying in the same tone,
"Ei n' it's grand ta meet thee n'all". This particular meeting was an agent back in the 1980's. After this awkward meet we just stared at each other for a while, and then after having a word with myself I said "cold isn't it though".......and carried on as normal, leaving him thinking "did that just happen"?

I had a teacher in my junior school, a lovely young woman who was Irish. It was one of the strongest accents I'd ever heard at the time. Oh dear it caused no end of confusion, I think at times she just thought I was being difficult, but I couldn't stop myself answering her in her own accent. The more annoyed she'd get the more I would panic and couldn't remember what I normally sounded like.

"Stop that nauuw ya nauuty giurl" she'd say. And with my eyes full to the brim with tears I'd reply,

"I'm truuying Miss I ruuarly am".

Eventually after a particularly bad case of this at the school Christmas party when I 'turrned rught aroind' during the Christmas carols concert, my Mum had to go to the school and meet with a bemused headmaster and the teacher in question the following day to explain,

"It's not you duckie, she doesn't mean to be disrespectful" she said looking down at me "she's like it all the time. How do ya think we feel? We have to live with it" said Mum. Er, thanks?

So back to long-time friend Karen, and I'm talking serious long-time friend. To inform you of how long, we met when we were 11 at Secondary School and have been friends since that class room introduction, I'm sure we will remain friends until our twilight years. She wasn't one of those 'fly by night sorts' that my Auntie Peg once spoke of. Not having a clue at the time what she meant, she described people who held this title as "they are the greatest of friends when they are with you, and then when you're not, you're out of sight, out of mind". I don't think this type of acquaintance mean any malice, but their brain probably works in the way of, they see something on TV, or walking through the park that reminds them of you, and then think "...oh I really must phone Shelley. I did promise last time I saw her in town that we must get together and..........ohhh look, a moth".

My Auntie Peg was right of course, not everyone is going to be playing a major role in your life's journey, and let's be honest now, that's a blessing sometimes!

Auntie Peg was a character, having to deal with serious illness since a little girl you'd be forgiven for thinking she may be of a miserable disposition, but actually she was the opposite. Quite easy going and liked a giggle. As she spoke to you she would whistle a cheery tune at the same time. "Oh hello duck *whistle* I hear your working *whistle* on the East Coast *whistle* next month" *whistle*.

But enough about Auntie whistles, bringing the chat back to school made pal however, Karen suggested "Why don't you come to mine after school, my Dad won't mind and we can go through me records".

So more often than not that's what would happen, I would test out a song in front of her and have some social time into the bargain.

Now then, 'that' just brought back a vivid memory of home, and the big wooden furniture unit we had that housed a record player! It had cupboards underneath, a glass cabinet over the top that held all Mum's very breakable glass treasures, a little open unit to the side, where a china lady lived, then a drop leaf door where the record player sat, complete with radio. You know something that highly polished unit may have been a bit bulky but the record player had one of the best sounds I've ever heard with its built in speakers, Radiogram? My Mum would nip round to a neighbours for a cuppa and Dad would say,
"Come on Blue let's get some hot toddy on!" Meaning rock and roll. Up would go the volume as Elvis or Tom Jones were belting out some classic. The bass in that unit was amazing.
I remember getting my first record player handed down from my older brother. Together with the built in wardrobe my Dad had made, pretty chair, white shelving unit, and small black and white TV, it made my bedroom complete, it was almost a bed-sit. I

practically lived in my bedroom, as did most of my friends hitting age 12/13, so when Mrs. Lamb (who lived next door) gave me a small electric kettle for my room she'd got free with Green Shield stamps, well, you couldn't touch me with a bargepole. Now I could actually make coffee in my room too. In my mind I would imagine I was one of the girls in 'Man About the House'........at what point does that innocence and imagination disappear? Playing my records in the evening and with my light on, I would knock the lampshade so that it swung from side to side, giving my room a 'disco feel'.....and the only room that had a fire was the sitting room, no central heating for the rest of the house!!! No wonder I used to dance a lot in my bedroom. 'Ei, we were frozen but we were happy'!

Friend Karen lived with her Dad and one evening I'd been at Karen's around an hour. We'd had a sandwich and drink and I asked where her Dad was.
"Oh he's doing something on the roof" she replied.
He was always busy with something so it wasn't really news. Top of the Pops came onto the TV and we sat watching and singing along. I distinctly remember 10cc being on and they were performing 'I'm Not in Love'. Half way through the song we just heard "arrrrrrrrrhhhhhhhhhhh".........*thud*, as I saw Karen's Dad, Freddie, fly past the window heading for the floor.
Honestly he was just a blur.
"KAREN, YOUR DAD, HE'S FALLEN OFF THE ROOF". I shouted.
"Oh not again" she said "he'll be alright". She then casually stood up and walked towards the window. Moments later in walked a disheveled Freddie dusting himself down as he walked into the sitting room saying,
"Have neither of ya put the kettle on"?
He was a one off.

Due to friendship and the choosing of songs I was often at Karen's and often her Dad would delight with another one of his Freddie mishaps.

One time Karen and I had been in town buying records and went back to her house. As we approached her house we spotted a new front door.

"Oh so that's what me Dad's been up to today is it" said Karen. As her key would no longer fit the new door we rang the doorbell. We heard a scuffle and mumbling inside and instructions of "push, push it"........so we both pushed the door to no avail. After five or ten minutes the door knocked us flying as Freddie realized he'd put it on back to front and it opened outwards.

That was actually the same day we were planted on the sofa listening to our newly purchased records and Karen's Dad after a full day of DIY popped his head around the door and announced, "right, I won't be long, I'm having a bath"........and off he went upstairs. He'd been up there 15-20 minutes and we heard *crash*. Karen ran to the bottom of the stairs,

"Dad! Dad!" she called, "Are you alright".

"Yeh" he called back "it's alright, I've just fallen out of the bath"................'Out' of the bath, how do you fall 'out' of a bath? But sure enough that's what had happened. Apparently he'd been reaching for the towel.

I'd go home after being at Karen's and my Dad would ask, "What's he been up to now" as I always seemed to have a story, it was almost like 'The Adventures of Freddie Fardell'. BBC you missed a treat there.

Popping round to Karen's one day, she said "Oh come in you won't believe this, it's all been happening here last night"

"Why, what's gone on" I asked.

"Well, you know how hot it's been? (It was the Summer of '76) He (she said looking over at her Dad) decides it's too hot to sleep under the covers so in the nuddy (nude) he's laying on top of the bed. Well did you hear that thunder storm we had in the early hours"?

"Yeh I did" I said, "My Mum came into my bedroom terrified saying my Dad didn't care there was a storm and he was just snoring all the way through it and not worrying about it at all". My Mum was very nervous of thunder storms.

Karen carried on "Well my Dad's laying there starkers on top of the bed, the thunder storm starts………he's in a deep sleep. It suddenly bangs and crashes and wakes him up, but because he's been in a deep sleep he thinks it's the end of the world, so stands up at the bedroom window where the curtains are wide open to get air from the open window and salutes. The woman across the road is looking out of 'her' bedroom window watching the storm and spots him and thought he was flashing at her". Without cracking a smile or batting an eyelid he just said, "Listen you pair I thought the world was ending and I just wanted to salute the Queen".

Old school manners, now you can't fault that can you.

I always enjoyed going to Karen's home, her Dad always made me feel very welcome and I always felt comfortable. You don't always get that in someone else's house, even when the owners make the right noises to welcome you in. But at Freddie's place you just did. I once went distraught as the careers teacher had crushed my career choices.

The career's teacher (had he been given that title under false pretences?) pushed and pushed for me to 'go into an office'….and I kept saying "but, I don't want to".

Not happy I hadn't agreed with 'his' choice he snarled,

"Well you're in a dream world and these silly pie in the sky ideas (ripping up my career choice paper) will never happen" he said leaning over his desk glaring at me.........quite intimidating.........nice. My three choices were (in no particular order) Vet, Midwife or Entertainer. The teacher laughed me out of the room basically, saying I wasn't suitable for any of my choices. So I went home that day with my tail between my legs.

With one of my choices I had to agree, as in agreeing after I'd had a very small taster. Vet..................no, oh dear me...................I lasted 45 minutes at the Veterinary Surgery where I'd been placed on work experience and they had to call my Dad to 'Collect Shelley, she's rather upset'.

But I did do my work experience at the City Hospital on the midwifery ward, and enjoyed it. OK, so I wasn't exposed to the serious reality side of things, I was 15, but I did enjoy it. The midwife I was guided by was great and the report I was sent back to school with was in my favour. I sang 'Happy Birthday' to the new born who arrived on my last day there........so maybe the entertainer bit was inevitable.

The following day of the careers 'advice' I'd been given, my Mum went to the school to 'have a word'.........Not sure what word that was exactly, but the careers teacher never spoke to me again, and would go as far as no eye contact when passing me in the corridor.

That evening I was at Karen's for tea and I told Freddie about it all............ He leaned on the arm of the chair looking at me until I'd finished, then after a sigh and shaking his head he said,

"If that's what you want to do then you do it duck, it's your life, don't let anyone push you into something you'd hate. You're the one that's got to live with it, not them".

Thank goodness I had some supportive grown ups surrounding me.

Out of the many Freddie misfortunes, one of my favourites actually, has to be 'Disappearing Freddie'……..where he had every man, woman and child out looking for him. I'd gone to Karen's and not seen her Dad all the time I was there. After a while I said, "Where's your Dad today".

"Oh he's gone to play golf" she said.

"Has he, has he walked it"? I asked.

"No, no, he's gone in the car" she replied.

"Are you sure? his car was parked outside when I arrived".

This was 2 hours previous.

We both looked out of the window and there stood Freddie's car.

"Well where is he then"? She said.

This was followed with a mass phone call to anyone and everyone who may have known where her Dad could be. No one came back with any useful information. There were no mobiles, it was the 1970's and so you either used the house phone or just waited for information to come to you.

I even phoned my Dad on the off chance he knew of his whereabouts. He didn't, but called round (Karen lived very close to me) to see if he could help.

Neighbour's were out in force and people were up and down the street trying to figure out where he could be. Karen was understandably very concerned and another hour had gone by. After a while a neighbour said,

"listen what's that noise"? We all went quiet and heard a dull 'thud, thud, thud' coming from inside Freddie's car. The neighbour said "It's coming from the boot. Quick Karen go and get his keys" he said, "where are the keys"?

Well, she hurried back claiming she couldn't find the keys. Eventually without too much damage my Dad and the neighbour managed to prize open the boot of the car…………and who lay there as neat as you please holding the car keys?............yes, Freddie. Various people moved forward to help him out.

"Dad" said Karen "You've had us worried sick, what ya doing in there"?

"Well, I thought me battery kept running down due to the light staying on in the boot, and so I thought 'if I shut myself in I'll be able to see if the light stays on'...............................and it does".

And with that he bypassed all of us, heading for the backdoor of the house rubbing his hands saying "I'm gasping for a cuppa".

Like many of our loved ones sadly Freddie is no longer with us, but the wealth of stories and his legacy of lunacy lives on. Thankfully I got to see him one more time before he drifted off to cause chaos in the heavens. He was exactly the same, I said to him,

"So, here we are, it's nice to see you, how's things then"?

He said "rubbish"..........Had one of 'the most' dry senses of humour I've ever come across, ahhhh just a straight talking pensioner.

After his funeral, for quite some time, Karen couldn't bring herself to scatter his ashes so she kept them at home.

During the sale of her house, she and her husband Mark were showing a couple around the house. Demonstrating the house with all of its benefits Mark was opening doors and cupboards to show how much storage there was. The tour arrived at the kitchen, "Mark went into overdrive" as Karen told me "opening every door in the kitchen to show off the amount of space there was for pots n' pans n' that".

Reaching the last cupboard Mark bends and opens it, only for the tour party to be greeted with one solitary item............the Urn of Freddie's ashes.

"Oh don't mind him" said Mark "that's just the father-in-law"!

.........................."VERY soon after this, the couple left" explained Karen when telling me the story "and not only that, we never heard from them again".

No..........................I don't suppose you would.

But I know for a fact Freddie would just love that he caused that hasty exit.

Are you lucky enough to know, or have known a Freddie?

Favourite overheard quote of the time.

"I was going to give blood yesterday afternoon but the place was shut so I went to TKMaxx instead."

Chapter Eight... Run Rabbit Run

Is it normal to break out into a cold sweat when a memory comes
back into your mind?

One very sunny summer season, (It rained just three days during
the whole season!) I found myself way down the south of England
on the North Devon coast, and what a pretty part of the country
it is too. It was all very laid back, the hustle and bustle that I'd
experienced previously in the cities and towns leading up to this
temporary seasonal move seemed a life time away.

I worked at a very nice resort where six evenings a week I would
walk down a pretty leafy lane with the sun peeping through the
kissing trees overhead, and together with my co-worker and
friend Jacqui we'd dance and sing our way through various shows.
Three main things I remember so vividly about this season was as
mentioned previously the constant sunshine. Other than the days
of childhood where Spring, Summer, Autumn and Winter were
exactly as ordered! This particular summer was exceptional for
the sunshine.

The second thing that springs to mind was my ankle. Arrhhh see
that's got your attention hasn't it. Well, either that or you've
just fallen asleep with the excitement. In which case you'll have
missed this too...........

One lucky reader gets a lifetime supply of..............

Oh, you woke up!

Back to ankle chat.........it had been a very busy week and the
guests were certainly out to party. Our visiting D.J. Richard was
a handsome sort and the ladies took quite a shine to him most
weeks but this week in question, they were rather, lets say,
obsessed with him. He was seriously worried for his safety, so
asked if Jacqui and I could help him to get out of the building
once he'd finished for the night.

"Are you serious"? asked Jacqui.

"Yes I am" Richard replied "If I can just get my things out as quickly as possible I don't think they'll be able to trap me"!
Oh aren't men dramatic.
As he packed his things away some of the ladies were hankering after goodnight, goodbye hugs and kisses and surprisingly the ones that had been 'full on' flirty on the dance floor just left by the main doors.
"I think you should be alright" said Jacqui to Richard.
"Uh, I'm not so sure. Why have the ones that have been all over me suddenly disappeared, I don't like it. It's all gone too quiet".
........Steady on lad, it wasn't Glastonbury!
Anyhow to put his little mind at rest Jacqui and I picked up various cases, boxes of his gear and all three of us headed outside into the balmy evening air to his parked van.
Not a lady-girl to be seen, all quiet on the western front. Or so we thought. As he opened the back doors to the van two 'girls' leapt forwards from inside the van and approximately 5 others came dashing from the bushes. It all happened very fast. With doors flying open and wild women to contend with Jacqui was last seen practically disappearing down the side gardens wishing well.....not something she'd wished for at all. Richard was being 'woman-handled' in the back of the van, with it appeared no escape. All you could hear were s-c-r-e-a-m-s of laughter, whoops, calls for help from our D.J. and basic noise, and despite all my efforts of trying to help him I'd been knocked to the ground (still holding onto the cases!) by the rather over-enthusiastic-should-know-better-at-that-age-fans. Oh ladies. Listen, been there, 'sort of' done that. But I was a teenager at the time, and I'd been screaming my head off for a popular band of the 70's (yay 'Flintlock') I admit, they stole my life for four years of it (see..... 'Carry Me Back to the 70's'). If any of these

ladies were likely to see 40 candles on their birthday cakes again, well…………???

I s'pose some reading this might think "Oh I bet he enjoyed it really", umm not so sure about that. Richard was a gentle young man and these women could be described as feral.

So laying there on the ground, still holding onto the cases…why? I was a bit dazed (and now I'm dazed at the thought of me still hanging onto the cases) but still unable to assist in the calls for help from our DJ pal. All of a sudden I heard Jacqui's voice, "I'll get security"……..and the hours went by! Well it sincerely felt like that, then just when you'd given up hope the black suits arrived and the ladies were dismantled back to, well, wherever they came from.

Richard was complimentary to the security chaps with admiration and relief. Jacqui was swearing like a trooper and demanding that security in future should…………secure. Then there was me…………I just sat for a while after being lifted like a sack of potatoes and perched on the garden bench. All was fine until I attempted the simple task of standing. Only ever having encountered not being able to stand in an upright fashion a few occasions previous during various birthday parties………hic! (….come on, we've all been there) this was rather worrying.

"Are you alright" asked Jacqui.

"I'm not sure" I said "I feel like my foot doesn't belong to me".

"Oh you've probably just got pins n needles or something, you'll be right" she assured me.

Together with my friend as a prop I limped my way up the leafy hill towards our shared caravan.

Jacqui was a true pal that evening, really taking care of my needs and helping all me all she could. We both convinced ourselves, a good night's sleep, plenty of rest for the foot and tomorrow all would be back to normal. And it was, that is until I woke up and naturally went to stand................YAAAAAAWWWWW. No, that's not going to happen. I couldn't put my shoe on, or a sock, or put any pressure what so ever on the now black and blue foot.

So the one day I could have done with his assistance he'd gone out for the day with wife Jean (Auntie) who was visiting. I refer to the keyboard player in the resident band, or I as know him 'Uncle Malcolm'. Well, he's not actually my uncle, but he almost is! You see, his brother was my uncle, is this confusing? I'll explain, my Dad's sister, married Malcolm's brother..........there.........that's cleared that up. Anyhow...............he wasn't there!

After a bit of faffing and trying to find someone who could take me to the hospital, a kind guest hearing Jacqui's pleas at the reception volunteered.

This will shock you but arriving at A&E and for such a small cottage hospital, I was the only one there (really) so was seen by a doctor immediately who said.........

"Arrhh, we just need to pop it back into place"

Who? What? What's being popped back into place?

Possibly me? Yes that's what it will be. 'I'm being popped back into the waiting room', I knew it wasn't that, but didn't like the sound of the alternative.

I obviously looked concerned as he said,

"No need to worry, we'll just pop it back and then after 24 hours rest and apart from some bruising you should be as good as new".

"Er, what are you popping back exactly"? I asked.

"Your ankle" he said with a smile "it's dislocated".

Eeewwww........."Isn't that going to hurt"? I asked, fully knowing what the answer was going to be.

"We-e-e-ll, you should be ok, it will be a matter of seconds" he replied.

This wasn't filling me with confidence.

"Can't you give me something"? I pushed "I don't know, a sedative, or vodka"............and we all laughed!

"Your quite chirpy" he said (damn that chirpiness) "I think you'll be fine".

You see its words like 'think' that didn't sit well for me, let alone stand.

He then did that thing that people have done to me for the whole of my career, the public that is. He looked at my info sheet and said,

"Arrrhhhh so you're a singer. There's a song I love, owww now how does it go?"

People do this............a lot. I have comedian friends who are constantly being told jokes by people........funny eh, or maybe not! I have quite a library of songs in my head, but even I don't know every song that's ever been recorded.

He carried on,

"Oh, you must know it, it goes Mmmm yeh, mm, mmmmMmmMMmm, don't you call me, mmMmm, yeh yeh, mmmmmmm"

Oddly enough nothing sprang to mind!

He then decided to repeat the whole thing, with other random words dotted about here and there, making the whole thing totally unrecognizable.

I smiled, "Er, no, no, nothing ringing any bells there I'm afraid" I politely said.

"Really?" He replied looking very surprised "It's really popular, well it was in the 60's, '68 I think it was, it's a great song, ohhhh what was the chorus bit".

He then tried to encourage the nurse to join in. Which was pointless, she looked about thirteen and of course she had even less of a clue than I did as to what this 60's classic was.

He carried on,

"Yehhh, umm mmmMmm, don't stop, yehhhh, mmMMmm".

I decided to nip it in the bud.

"Ohhhh, I bet you'll remember it all later in the day when you're not thinking about it" I said trying to hurry proceedings along.

"Your probably right" he said "though it's a shame you don't know it. It's a real foot tapper".

A real 'foot' tapper was it. Was he having a laugh?!

"If I remember it during the night expect a phone call at 4am" he said laughing.

Comedian doctor eh........why me?

Anyhow the nurse then walked over to me with a plastic shallow bowl and stood at my left hand side with her arm around my shoulder and bowl just within heaving distance.

"Ei, Ei" I thought, "here we go then".

"OK Shelley" said Doctor Casual Sing-a-Lot "let's get this back to its rightful place".

"Ooo Kaayy" I said whilst shaking my head in a 'no' fashion.

He then glanced at the nurse, looked at me and said,

"Right then, here we go after three, one...two"....CLUNK.

How very cheeky going 'on' three and not after three. His doctoring skills exceeded his singing skills, thankfully.

........And there it was done.......Didn't hurt...........Nah, nothing to it. It was just a regular dislocated ankle.........anyone reading convinced?

All I will say is, if you ever find yourself with a dislocated ankle, just get it popped back in, it stings a bit, but the alternative isn't attractive.

"There you go" he proudly announced "all done, how you feeling"?

"Like I want to scream, but I won't ha ha ha ha hee hee ha ha hee hee ha ha ha hee hee hee................." I said, and I carried on laughing in a very strange delirious manner. After twenty minutes had passed and I'd run out of laughs, things calmed down and I was allowed to leave with the promise of strong painkillers to pick up via my exit and 24 hours rest.

The kind guest then took me back to my mobile home and for some unknown reason decided to tell me about every hospital procedure he'd ever had during his lifetime. I believe his misguided chat had in fact been in an attempt to sooth my distressful experience by letting me know 'you're not the only one'. It didn't, but it's the thought that counts eh.

When I got back sweet Jacqui was waiting with the kettle on, and on informing anyone that would listen during the morning of my A&E absence, folk had been very kind, therefore a bunch of flowers and overpriced chocolates were also waiting for me.

It was in the afternoon with windows open and sofa rest for 'herself' that the third memory was made.

As I lay there getting instructed rest, I heard two of the staff outside talking about the 'petting area'. Owww now then, that got your attention. Possibly got your mind wandering? Now then, don't be saucy! The venue wasn't crossed with a 'Carry On' film. The 'petting area' was where people could go and see the guinea pigs, birds etc and a beautiful lop eared rabbit.

I was familiar with this area as from day 3 after arriving I discovered it and would go and fuss the animals and generally sit and watch the lovely birds as they flew around the aviary.

The rabbit (that I named 'Thumper') seemed so sad. It would just sit in the outside run of its hutch, and look at the ground, only moving now and again. The only time I saw the poor thing take any interest in life was when I began to go first thing in the morning and take a carrot with me. Even then it was such a big effort for him/her to come over to me at the edge of the enclosure. It used to upset me so much to see it so unhappy.

Just when I thought my unhappy feelings couldn't get any unhappier, I overheard the two staff members saying how at the end of the season the guinea pigs and the rabbit were going to be 'let go'..........Let go? 'What does that mean exactly'? I thought. I pulled myself up so that I could look out of the caravan window and called over to the two men,

"Oi, come here, I want to ask you something".

One of the men walked over to the caravan.

"Sorry for being nosey" I said (I wasn't sorry at all) "But what did you mean by the animals are going to be 'let go' at the end of season"?

"Oh right, you are nosey aren't ya" said the chap "The animals are going to be let go into the wild when season finishes, that's all" he said.

THAT'S ALL......'that's terrible' I thought.

"That can't happen" I said "These animals are domesticated, you can't expect them to survive in the wild, they'll be killed".

"Well it will happen. Not my rules love, if you've got a problem with that then your best to talk to the general manager".

I felt awful, and the moment Jacqui got back I told her what I'd heard.

"Really?" she said "are you sure they weren't just winding you up. I can't believe they'd let the animals just go, why would they do that, it's just plain cruel".

And my rest and recuperation time had disappeared into insignificance. All I could focus on was the poor animals.

There was only four weeks left of the season so if I was to stop this from happening I had my work cut out.

It was two nights later Jacqui and I pinned down the G.M. as he stood at the bar entertaining two over groomed gents. He ushered us away from the bar and said gents and once we arrived at a safe distance he asked what was wrong and we both questioned him about what we'd heard about the animals being 'let go' at the end of season.

"Yeh, that's right, got a problem with that girls have you"? He said laughing.

"Well, yes, we have, well I have", I said. "That's terrible you know they'll be killed within 24 hours?"

"Well I can't believe your being serious, you're not being serious are you?" Jacqui said "You can't do this, they'll die".

"Ohhh it's only a rabbit and a few rats" he said with his continuing laugh. "Girls there are far more serious things to worry about".

"Their domesticated animals" I pleaded.

"................look girls I don't have time for this".........he said glancing around the room, and then he strolled back dismissing us with his hand and saying something to the effect of 'over emotional women'.

The pure fact he'd finished any sort of conversation he was going to have with us about the animals, ending in 'I don't have time for this' kinda summed it all up really.

Jacqui and I sat back stage talking it all through and saying how rude he'd been, not to even give us a valid reason. It was then we came up with our master plan. On the last night of the season, we'd rescue them! Yes, that could be phrased as another word for steal.

The birds fortunately were being collected by a lady who owned an even bigger aviary a few miles away. We found this out the very next day as we saw her and her husband arrive with cage after cage in the back of a large van. Lovingly one by one she caught the birds and placed them gently into the cages with promises of a new home.

I stood there watching and trying to persuade her to take the bunny and guinea pigs too.

"Oh I can't dear" she said "much as I'd like to, I have four huge aviaries and I just don't have the room with our 3 dogs too"

So I sensibly begged. It still didn't sway her to take them.

Over the next week or so, rumours came back to our ears that the G.M. had been taking the mickey out of mine and Jacqui's pleas of 'don't do this to the animals', saying "my animals, I'll do what I like". Ummm.

Two weeks to the end of season and I was on the phone to home…. H-o-o-mmeee (that was my best ET impression, no, no more, that's ya lot).

I was telling my Mum all about the pet-problem and began getting upset.

"Oh duckie, you do worry me all the way down there and being so upset, here talk to ya Dad".

He came on the phone "What's up ma duck".

Knowing how much my Dad also loved animals I went into the full story of the petting area and the 'letting go' saga.

"Oww that's not rate is it ma duck" he said "so what's ya plan".

Firstly how did he know I even had a plan swirling about in my head?

"Well, we thought we'd just er……………take them"………………………….

(I said it as fast as I could knowing it was……………er…………wrong)

I stood on the other end of the phone waiting for the dressing down of how I shouldn't do that.

But the reply that came back was,

"Right then, so you'll need some boxes and a cage" Yee! Go Dad!

We were/are a law abiding family by the way, this was extenuating circumstances.

The next weekend via a family friend on holiday, a small dog basket arrived and a selection of small boxes, the proper animal safe ones with holes in them. My Dad knew someone for every occasion!

Jacqui had set up travel plans to get us back home in the form of her brothers, and after explaining to them about our plan they hired a large van to take us, a season's worth of 'stuff' and the animals all back to Nottingham.

"Right, we've only got one chance to do this" said Jacqui, so we actually wrote down a plan of action. As I type this I'm sitting giggling at the memory, not because of the thought of rescuing the animals, just the detail we went to, to do it in the first place. Mission impossible, nope, anything's possible.

The final evening arrived. I'd felt sick all day, and it was like the 'League of Gentlemen' (Have you ever seen that film where several gents were planning a bank robbery?). Each time I caught Jacqui's eye we'd just sort of look, and nod. There were no smiles, just pursed lips and nods of reassurance towards each other. The last evening was a little like a gala event. Lots of returning guests, cabaret, plus our D.J. the lovely Richard (complete with personal security, his brother). It was a real party atmosphere.

Meanwhile back in Nottingham my Dad had been busy. Finding potential adopted families for the guinea pigs (all 8 of them) and building a hutch for 'Thumper'.

I called home during the afternoon.

"Ow hello duckie" said my Mum on the phone "Ya Dad's busy outside, he's made this hutch for the bunny, I'll tell ya, poor little thing is going to feel lost in it, even 'I' can get inside it, you know what ya Dad's like when he starts building something"……….

But I wasn't bothered, it could have been as big as our own house, just knowing 'Thumper' had a safe place once we were back home was all I was concerned about.

Mum carried on "...anyway, you be careful, oww duckie you do worry me. Oh yes I need to say while I remember I've made an appointment at Tuesday morning at the vets, 10 o'clock, ya Dad thinks Thumper should be checked by somebody just to be on the safe side duckie".

I came off the phone and my stomach was doing cart wheels. It was real now..........this time tomorrow we'd be in a van traveling north, no turning back now.

End of seasons, like touring shows, pantos..........if you've had a good one that is.........are always quite emotional. Chances are even though you've become so familiar with people in a relatively short space of time and for want of a better phrase have become as close as family, it's highly unlikely you'll ever share those experiences with them again, and in some cases, never see those people again. Guests also are in that factor, some people you just click with.

As well as the 'one off' afternoon show on our last day, during the evening Jacqui and I danced and sang our way through an artiste filled cabaret show, sharing the stage with the likes of singer Paul DaVinci and ventriloquist Neville King to name but two, also doing their bit. The audience seemed to have a fabulous time and as the balloons fell from the ceiling the champagne flowed like water.

Midnight arrived........apart from the D.J. and bar staff, everyone was out to party. It was a fabulous atmosphere, but one Jacqui and I couldn't share for too long. We hung around and subtly said our goodbyes and gave out cheerio hugs so not to arouse suspicion.

1.30am came and the party was still in full swing, Jacqui and I decided to depart the party and just made a very quiet exit out through the back stage entrance picking up our costumes and bags on the way. Outside some of the staff we're packing their cars ahead of doing a night time drive back to their respective homes around the country, so we bid them a goodnight and just said how we were shattered and had an early start so wanted to get back for some sleep.

Once back in the caravan off came the glitz and glamour and on went the black track suits and bobble hats. Yes, we did don that clothing. Just past 2.30am and we'd heard quite a few cars leave, all went quiet so we thought we'd jump into action.

Out of the caravan and over the small field........it was pitch black and I suddenly heard Jacqui say in the darkness,

"Ohhhh nooooo, I've just stepped in something, and I don't think its sugar".......

That sort of comment would usually have had me giggling, especially at 2.30am in pitch black in a field in the middle of the night (not that being in a field in pitch black in the middle of the night was a regular thing!) But due to the whole reason why we were in that situation I just said

"We'll wipe it off with a damp cloth when we get back". I can be surprisingly sensible.

All of a sudden we noticed the full beam head lights of a car coming up the hill from the venue, so we bobbed down on the grass and kept as still as we possibly could.

"Has it gone"? said Jacqui.

"I don't know? I've got my eyes shut" I said.

Before we knew it, it had gone and we heard the car's engine as it disappeared down the country road.

We made it across the field and then climbed over the fence into the petting area. All the animals were awake and thinking we'd taken food treats were eager to come up to us.

So over I climbed into their rickety enclosure.

"Pass us a guinea pig" said Jacqui "I'll put one in this box".

Not something you hear everyday, but I did and taking out a box from the black bin liner she'd had over her shoulder, she carefully placed it in.

"One down, seven to go" She said.

I corrected her "........and 'Thumper'"

"Oh yeh, but I think you'd better pick him up, you've fed him, he knows you" (we presumed due to his size it was a 'he').

One by one we got all the guinea pigs in their respective boxes. Then it was 'Thumpers' turn. I clambered over into the run (I say run...you'd have struggled to get a walk out of it)

"Come on sweetie" I said, and the docile bunny just hopped into my arms.

"Owwwww bless him" said Jacqui "I think he knows were helping". I felt that way too. As I lifted him up, he just closed his eyes and I had his full weight, he'd totally relaxed.

'I hope that hutch is big enough Dad' were my thoughts.

'Thumper' sure was a 'big lad'.

The next few hours in the caravan were entertaining to say the least. We'd made a little enclosure of our own with cushions for the guinea pigs to have a scuttle about and Thumper was up and down the corridor and he kept making little 'ee'ee' sounds each time I stroked him, he loved it. It was the liveliest I'd seen him in the whole season. We didn't sleep at all. We'd previously decided to keep alert knowing we had to keep an eye on the animals plus a very early morning call.

Just before 4.30am we decided to get the fur-babys back into the boxes and ready for the off, knowing this wasn't going to be a quick job we wanted it all to be as calm as possible. By the time I'd put Thumper back into the basket I'd downed a number of coffees, which was handy as I know where I am after three coffees, before that I'm just walking into walls.

5am came and just after as Jackie was sweeping the floor a knock at the door. My heart stopped for a split second.

Jacqui pulled back the curtain, "It's alright, it's my brothers", she confirmed.

I opened the door to two big strapping fellows, resembling the Mitchell brothers from 'Eastenders', the taller of the two said "A-up duck, I'm Jac's brother, ya got all ya stuff n these 'ere animals ready then, sooner we get off the better".

"Yeh, we're all sorted" I said, quite excited at the promise of the escape.

Jacqui hugged her brothers and then with all basic intros done and the light starting to break, the birds began chatting to each other as we all loaded up the van. By 5.30am we were waving goodbye to our caravan.

"Bye caravan" yes, we actually said it (don't sit there looking all innocent you know you've said goodbye to mundane things too). Through the main gate and that was that, moving further and further down the lane until we could no longer see it, we were on our way.

Three hours later we had a little water stop and checked on the furry friends. Jacqui's brothers had bought some golden delicious apples for the animals in case they needed a snack, how sweet was that. I bit one in half and 'Thumper' savoured every mouthful of his half.

"Aye's rate enjoyin' that apple" said one of the brothers. These lads were real 'bruisers', but soft as anything. Jacqui checked on the guinea pigs and with everyone watered, humans included, we carried on with our journey.

We did so well with our travel time, and by mid afternoon were pulling up outside my home in Nottingham.

My Dad came out of the house and with several trips he'd carried back inside boxes of guinea pigs and various items of my luggage.

Jacqui and I hugged and shared a few tears. It hadn't just been an emotional season but a highly emotional 24 hours. Then I waved them off and walked into the house with my dog basket and new friend.

"Let's have a look at him then" said Mum "Oh bless him, look at that little face. Let ya Dad take him to his hutch duckie and I'll make you a drink".

I have no idea why but I just burst into tears! (yeh, again).

"Eh, now stop that" said Mum "You've done a lovely thing today, it's probably a bit illegal as well duckie, but it's all for the right reasons"!!!

We then heard my Dad say "A-up 'ayes' lovin' it" and both Mum and I, followed by the dog, went outside to see 'Thumper' in his new home. Dad was right to make it as high as it was wide as on getting outside 'Thumper' spotted me and stood on his hind legs and reached almost to the top of the hutch.

"I wa' rate about that hutch, I knew 'ayed be a big un" said Dad. It was a beautiful hutch with a bedroom area and all fresh straw making a lovely comfortable bed, new dishes and if I'm honest, I wouldn't have minded living there myself, rather posh as hutches go. If rabbits could rate hutches, then I'm sure 'Thumper' would've rated 'his' 5 star........or.........9 carrots!

The following day various people (who'd been vetted by Mum) came to collect Tommy, Sausage, Pompom, and other Guinea pig individuals that Mum had felt the need to name, and we took 'Thumper' to the vets. It cost us quite a pretty penny (even back then) as she needed booster jabs, had an infection in her ears, a fungus on her feet and was infested with fleas..........but she was worth every penny. Yes, you did read that correct, he was in fact a 'she', Thumper'ess if you will. The vet said how she'd been neglected for quite some time but with some TLC chances are we could keep her for another 6 months possibly with a bit of luck a year as she was quite the elderly lady (you know what's coming next don't you……….'and cue the tears'). You can take your hands away from your eyes now, of course there was no question of anything else happening, so we 'all' went back home and over the next few weeks she had around the clock care from the parents and I. After a week we saw a positive change in her, she began to groom herself again and after two weeks, she was like a different bunny. Her coat was beautiful, her eyes bright, and Dad had made a rabbit run the length, just about, of the garden, and boy could that bunny hop. Mum had a dwarf rabbit called 'Silver', and he was very interested, a bit too interested if you know what I mean, *nudge nudge*. Mum insisting the rabbits have exercise at different times as she didn't want to be over run with dwarf rabbits with lop ears!!!

Word came back to me via Uncle Malcolm that the G.M. has said the following year "that Shelley, she knicked our rabbit"…………
well, he couldn't have been that bothered. All of my information was on file. It would have been the simplest thing to track me down. I think he was thankful he didn't have to deal with the animal's full stop.

Very kindly Mum and Dad looked after 'Thumper' as my work was taking me all over Europe, but they didn't mind.

And Thumper………….well, if the vet's assessment was correct which I believe it was and Thumper was an elderly lady……she exceeded the 6 months to a year expectation, and we had her as part of the family for just short of another 3 years.

Not that I'm suggesting you go and steal a rabbit……No……but for me, it was one of the best things I've ever done.

So have you ever done something outrageous to save/protect an animal?

Favourite overheard quote of the time.

"...Hello my dear, can you tell me what time the midnight disco starts!"

Chapter Nine... I Think I Love You

Have I mentioned I'd been a fan of David Cassidy for a few
years! ☺ It all began when I was ten years old. Saturday early
evening and a new programme had been introduced on the TV
called 'The Partridge Family', I remember the posh continuity
announcer had described it as 'a story with music'. 'Well lead me
towards the TV then", we were onto a winner the moment she
said 'music'.

It opened up with a pop song...."Hello world there's a song that
we're singin', COME ON GET HAPPY......." It did actually make you
happy. It was bright and cheerful, and even though at the time
we only had a black and white TV, for me that didn't matter it
was already colourful through the eyes of a ten year old. Then it
happened.................... 'his' face appeared on the screen. (*angels
sing on high*) Keith Partridge's face that is, and that particular
afternoon that was all I knew of him, but that was all I needed
to know. Not quite sure what the story was about, my focus of
interest was to just look at his pretty face.......! Yes 'Keith' was
soooo pretty, so pretty in fact that I became completely
addicted to this show, having to watch each and every episode
that followed. Keith was of course David Cassidy....or to use his
full title, 'David my first love Cassidy'!

Apart from the weekly Partridge fix, various magazines and of
course Top of the Pops, my love affair with David could go no
further than TV and magazines. The possibility of going to one of
his concerts was a definite no-no. I actually sat and worked out
how old he would be once I'd reached 21 and was able to marry
him! But as far as concerts were concerned, "no, you're far too
young" Mum insisted.

Funny isn't it what memories you keep with you without even
making a conscious effort to save them, and even though they

don't blow your mind, they seem to have set up camp in your memory banks. When I think back to that time I can clearly see my Dad sitting in his chair watching the wrestling on a Saturday afternoon...............1'a, 2'a, 3'a.............we would also join in with the countdown once the likes of Giant Haystacks, Big Daddy or Jackie Pallo had hit the canvas.

The other thing would be, all of us glued to the TV on a Sunday afternoon for 'The Golden Shot'.

"Up a bit, down a bit, right a bit"........and that was only us guiding Dad holding up the TV aerial!

However I spent so much time in my bedroom, playing records, writing, making 'things' etc, so it was very important from the off that Mum knew to give me a shout when the Partridge Family was about to start. There were three regular 'calls' from downstairs in order to get my attention.

Firstly......"HE'S ON", with the aim (always a successful one) to draw me downstairs to watch 'The Partridge Family'.

Secondly..."Shelley 'Pa-pah-dahs on with that girl who keeps crying". Mum would be referring to the programme 'Follyfoot', and for those of you who are confused by the 'Pa-pah-dahs' bit, well that was the opening theme music 'The Lightning Tree'.

The third thing would be,
"TURN IT DOWN"............when my volume on the record player had accidentally slid to number 10 from number 5.......It's easily done.

As the years went by and the fashion of who was in vogue and who was out changed, like many who had followed him since we all met up on that multi-coloured bus, David always had a place in my

heart. Those eyes, that face, the unique beautiful
voice...Ow sorry, lost
concentration for a moment there.

So having never seen him live I just did like many fans world
wide, I collected the records and the pictures. There was no
internet, you couldn't just look him up on Youtube.

It wasn't until January in 2001 that I went to Las Vegas with
the husband for a little holiday. I'd already pre-booked to see
'At the Copa' (which was nothing to do with Mr. Manilow) but a
show that starred David Cassidy and Sheena Easton. This was
going to be the first time I'd ever seen David 'live'.

During the 1980's and 90's due to my career, whenever he'd been
over in the U.K. touring it had never been convenient to go to a
concert

The flight itself over to the U.S.A. was as entertaining as actual
Vegas. Approaching San Francisco the pilot announced,

"OK, for those of you on the right hand side of the plane, if you
look out of your windows you'll see the impressive Golden Gate
Bridge, and for those of you on the left hand side of the plane
you can look at the people on the right hand side looking out of
their windows at the bridge"..........ha ha, love it.

Vegas really 'is' another world. Some refer to it as the
entertainment capital and others say it's tacky, if that is the
case then it's the most expensive tacky I've ever seen.

That aside, I think if you're in the entertainment business
especially, you should treat yourself with a visit and make your
own opinion, it really is like nothing else.

Landing in Vegas there is an unmistakable atmosphere, very
glitzy and grand. As it was January you could tell in an instant
who the locals were, all walking around with thick coats on, yet
the Europeans were casually walking around in jeans and cotton

tops. Their winter is the equivalent, in weather terms, to a bright spring day in the U.K.

Each hotel is a small town within itself, hosting fabulous bands and entertainment. The hotel we stayed at, 'The Excalibur' being a prime example. One of our resident bands called 'Souled Out', were amazing, such a talented bunch of musicians, yet one evening there couldn't have been more than 20 of us in the audience.

It is a gambling capital and so as you entered the hotel there was this clang clang clang, ching ching ching on a constant loop as the sound of a couple of hundred one arm bandits and gambling machines rattled around the huge foyer. It was overwhelming to start with, but believe it or not after the first 24 hours your ears get used to the noise and you don't hear it so much.

Within a few hours of landing we'd checked into our hotel, and had a rather large late lunch! It made dinner time at home look like a snack. We walked around the area surrounding our hotel, popped into various bars, then back to the hotel watched some TV, and the following day as we stood in Starbucks waiting for a coffee, who was in the queue in front of us, only 'Duran, Duran's' John Taylor. He was lovely, very friendly and on hearing we were 'Brits' spent time chatting, not too shabby on the eye either girls.

That same evening we left our hotel and stood waiting in the taxi cab queue as we were heading for 'The Rio' the hotel which was host to the show, 'At The Copa'. The queue went down quickly and at the point where our cab arrived the smart uniformed attendant opened the door for us and said "Hey guys welcome to Vegas, we gotta celebrity here", we both got into the taxi.

"What does he mean"? I asked Alan "I don't know" he said "P'raps it's just something they say"?

We arrived at the Rio and handing our tickets in at the door to the theatre we were led by our host through the room which was on a gradual slant leading down to the stage. The room was huge. We kept following him further and further down towards the stage.

"Wow, I didn't realize how good the seats were going to be when I booked them over the phone" I said.

"Yep" said our guide "You guys are practically on the God dam' stage".

And we were. Table 17, which sat as part of the second row of tables directly in front of centre stage. Each tiny round table had 4 chairs surrounding it, and Alan and I shared our table with a young woman from Houston, Texas. Her name was Holly and she was there with her friend. We immediately introduced ourselves to one another and instantly jelled, chatting about our common interest. Like yours truely neither of the girls had seen David 'live' before, but had been dedicated fans since the Partridge Family days.

This evening took me back to seeing my favourite band back in my teenage days, as I was so very excited. It was the same feeling I'd experienced years ago at their first concert.

As I glanced around the room I could see lots of people, mainly women with t-shirts on with the shows logo on or pictures of David. I'd witnessed this in my teens, heck I'd done this in my teens, and more, but never seen 'women' in so many numbers sporting a similar style. It was quite sweet. I on the other hand had gone out and out Vegas with a sequin top and shiny trousers and jacket..........Well, if you can't do bling in Vegas when can you! I suddenly realized two people on the table right at the side of us were just staring. I glanced behind me and smiled.

"I think they're looking at you" said Holly.

"Yeh, definitely staring right at you" confirmed her friend.

Then the show began, the room cheered, many screamed through sheer anticipation of what was to come. The Lon Bronson Orchestra played and the stage lights dimmed and then..................cue Mr. Cassidy.

'Oh look, there he is, I think? Is it him'?

It was slightly odd to begin with, with dim lights David appeared on the stage but he was disguised as an old man! But this didn't deter the ladies in the audience. This was a musical play, not a concert, but you wouldn't have known, the women screamed the place down. After the 'old fella' finished his speech the show began and sexy young ladies danced across the stage to Sheena singing and then there he was, now de-robed of the old chap look, yes, there he was indeed, the object of my desire, ever since I'd realized what the word desire meant all those years ago.......David.

It wasn't the 1970's anymore, but in 2001, David still looked mighty fine.

Our seats were so close to the stage that we had the most perfect view of the stage, the band and most importantly of him. I glanced across at Holly and just like me she had the biggest smile on her face. The taking of photographs wasn't allowed, but that was ok really. Who wanted to look through a piece of plastic and glass at this beautiful man when you could just be there with him in the actual moment.

He began to sing and sounded as fabulous as he had done all those times I'd played his records, cassettes, CD's........such a fabulous unmistakably unique husky voice.

As it was a musical play, David's own hits weren't the main attraction, but it was a great show with a nice mix of music. During the show however we did get a treat of a few of David's trademark hit songs starting with 'I Think I Love You' which made the sell out crowd cheer with great enthusiasm. As if this

wasn't just fabulous in itself he then began to walk to the side of the stage where there were steps and walked down into the audience, this was really happening, whoopee.

The security seeped from either side of the room to keep an eye on the crowd, David's stroll into the audience causing great excitement. He walked from one table to another, singing and shaking hands as he did so. He was getting closer, and closer, and.............he was at the table in front of us..........right there, touch-a-ble close. He stood with his back to our table singing "I don't know what I'm up against, I don't know what it's all about...etc....................", and then spun around singing "Hey I think I love you" holding out his hand to me............ME!

I hadn't 'thought' I loved him for years, I 'knew' I loved him. I also knew this may be my only chance of letting him know! So taking hold of his hand I stood up, threw my arms around him, hugged and kissed him, and hugged him some more. What husband? David looked over my shoulder at Alan and said "Arhhh I see, this is a kinda kissing night yeh". He was wearing Paco Raban aftershave, Paco Raban baby! I left the most perfect pink 'kiss' shape imprint on his cheek, talk about leaving your mark. Knowing my place, and being of sound mind, (*cough*) I then sat back down, but didn't let go of his hand, in fact by now I was holding his hand with both of mine. He stood at our table singing while I gently stroked his hand looking lovingly into those eyes............................. ....sorry, there I go again, drifted off for a while then, arrrrhhhhhhhhhh.

I was very lucky, he stood for quite some time, just letting me have my cuddles and he just waved to others further back in the room. Thankfully Holly and friend also got some David lovin', and then he made his way back onto the stage. He finished the song with my pink lip sweetheart kiss stamped on his face, and then left the stage. When he returned to do another song it had been rubbed off..........what a cheek!!!

The show was fabulous from start to finish. As it ended the cast stood taking their bows and a few glanced over at our table. We waved and cheered, we'd had a fantastic night.

After the show, we said our goodbyes to the girls and then went to another part of the hotel for a drink. The bar we found was rather unusual in that it had a trapeze act in it. There was a large oblong bar and after ordering our drinks the husband decided he needed the loo, so off he went in search of one.

I sat at the bar on my own, but within minutes of being on my own I could see I was being watched by two couples..............and they carried on watching me.

It felt a little awkward so I smiled..........and that was it, they quickly gathered up their things and rushed over to me.

"Hiiiiiiiiii" said one of the ladies.

"Ohhhh myyyyy Godddddd" said the other lady.

"We caaant believe it's yooooou" they both announced in very strong American accents.

"Eh"? I replied.

"Ohhhh youuuuu" said one of the ladies "We know who you arrre".

"Eh"? I said again.

"Oh myyyyy your so funnyyyyy", said the other lady "Quick, let me get a pen".

I had no idea what was going on. The lady dipped into her bag held by her smiling husband and on finding a pen and programme said to me........

"Honey could you be a sweedie and sign this to Phyllis".

"Eh"? I said yet again.....who says those drama lessons were a waste!

I felt the need to make a statement for the excitable foursome.

I smiled "Erm, I'm so sorry, but I'm not who you think I am. I think there's a case of mistaken identity here, I wasn't in the show", I emphasized, thinking to myself, 'well that's got that all sorted'.

"Ohhhh your hysterical", said one of the men "we know who you arrrrrre".

"Oh but you don't", I said.

"Oh we do, oh look at herrr, she's such a kidder. We love you, could you sign this"? Said the most forceful of the two ladies. They all stood grinning at me, waiting..........so, I just.........signed.........it was easier, and they were so grateful.

I continued to do a couple more signings! And as my husband returned from the gents I was having group photographs taken. As he approached me with the most confused look on his face, he mouthed "What on earth are you doing"?

The autograph hunters gave me their thanks, hugs and kisses, and off on their jolly way they went waving and calling 'love you', way into the distance until they went through some double doors and I could see them no more.

"I've only been gone ten minutes, what was that all about", he asked.

"Well" I said "They think I'm someone famous that they know, obviously I'm not, but they wouldn't hear of it, so it was just easier to sign autographs and have photos taken, and they're happy so.............."

I've often wondered if they got home and looking at their photos at some point in the future thought "who is that, that's not such-n-such". It's something I'll never know, but for me it made a very special memorable evening even more memorable.

On returning home and telling the tale to a few friends, some who had frequented visits to the states said how I resembled a daytime soap actress, also English, so this may have caused the confusion. If it wasn't that, then like you, I don't have the foggiest.

After that initial first sighting of D.C. in Vegas, whenever possible during the 'noughties', meeting up with friends I traveled to see him in concerts and personal appearances over here in England. My love of all things David has given me lovely friends Sharon, Elaine, Krysia, (all three of them from England), Tereza (Brasil), Marion (Germany), Clara and Theresa (U.S.A.) and many more besides.

...And of course Holly, She may be thousands of miles away, but we haven't lost contact with one another either. Ever since our two visits to see 'At The Copa', at the second show we exchanged addresses and through post, email and later on Facebook we have kept in touch ever since. Once again, just like the 1970's gave me great friends following the group 'Flintlock', I have a friend I wouldn't have otherwise met, all down to the power of music....oh and a beautiful face, let's not forget David's lovely face.
Sadly David Cassidy passed away in November 2017.........one of the saddest times ever for me personally and also for my like-minded friends. It was difficult news to take in. I still can't believe he's gone. Whether he was to your taste or not, I'm sure you can appreciate how hard it is when someone has been there taking a dominant role in your life story for the best part of it, regardless of if you see them everyday, or not................I'm glad he was here in my lifetime.

Have you ever been mistaken for someone else?

Favourite overheard quote of the time.

"I just can't get her attention. She obviously can't hear me over that stupid hairstyle."

Chapter Ten... Take Me I'm Yours

Sometimes, just every now and again, for the smallest of reasons, life can be quite disappointing cant it. Example, I'd just got home from a gig and turned on the TV. I was quite thrilled when I heard the continuity announcer say "Well that's the weather..........and now music with Abba followed by Darts".
"Oh great" I thought. Even though the back to back line up did seem a little 'out there', I settled with a snack on the sofa to watch an hour of Abba, swiftly followed by Darts. Imagine my disappointment when instead of looking at a very eclectic line up of individuals making up the band 'Darts' and hearing the tones of 'Come Back My Love'......I was confronted with Jockey Wilson, actually throwing darts. As I said, disappointing.

So, we all know there is an opposite of everything, so for everything that's disappointing, there has to be moments of glee. Gleeness even..........*puts coffee down and walks over to dictionary to look up the word gleeness..............decides before picking up the dictionary its highly unlikely the word gleeness exists.........walks back, picks up coffee*.
Anyhow, as I was saying, if you have disappointment, then chances are you will have moments of gleeful'ness. (I'm past caring, report me to the word inventors!)

Ahh disappointments............due to my line of work, I'd have to say missing out on friends birthday celebrations, weddings, christenings and even funerals in the past has been disappointing. The latter might seem an odd thing to miss, but when you haven't had the chance to say goodbye or support a family member or friend, it can weigh heavy on your heart.

Weddings, well they fall into the category of 'Isn't it great something nice is happening'.

My friend Caroline married while I was working away in some distant land, so sadly I missed her wedding day. My Mum became my dep and told me all about the day via letters and photos. By the time my contract was up and I'd returned Caroline had moved her life and husband up to the highlands of Scotland.

When she lived in Nottingham, we sure had some wild times (If anyone should have hold of any negatives by the way, I'm sure we can come to some sort of arrangement!) ☺

Some of the more controlled outings, theatre and meals out for example would often involve having our mothers in tow, happy times.

After 1990 with my Mum no longer around and Caroline up in Scotland, it didn't mean I couldn't see Caroline's Mum, Anne. So I would meet her now and again when I'd pop back to Nottingham to visit family. We would catch up over lunch or a coffee. She missed my Mum so much, they were great pals and so I think it gave us both the chance to chat about her through our shared memories.

While 'home' on one occasion after failing miserably to land an audition for a 40's show due to my age, then 32! I'd suddenly found myself with 3 days free so I'd arranged to meet Anne (Mum II) outside the Theatre Royal in Nottingham.

"Meet me on steps, we go for lunch yes" she said when I'd phoned her the day before "I don't want miss you".

"You won't miss me 'Mum' I'll be dressed head to toe in purple" I said

"Persil"?........."why you wear Persil" she asked.

I chuckled down the phone....."no, not Persil, purple, pur-ple" I said exaggerating the purrr and ple.

Anne was German and her fluent but broken English would often have us, my Mum in particular, in stitches. You could be in the middle of a busy street with Caroline and Anne walking ahead of my Mum and I and you'd suddenly hear "MUM hee hee hee hee"...and Anne would've come out with a classic 'Anne line'.

She was once in Boots with my Mum (do I get triple points with all these plugs for the shop?) wanting to buy Caroline some perfume for her birthday. She asked the girl at the perfumery counter,

"I need perfume for Caroline it's her birthday you know, please, a bottle of incest"..........

"Ohhh no, no, no Anne" said my Mum quickly jumping in the conversation to clear up any misunderstanding! I recall Mum saying to me,

"Ohhhh, you should've seen the look on the girls face, oh I do love Anne". She would often get her words mixed up, it was rather endearing.

There is a Nottingham slang word called 'Scrating' (pronounced scray-ting)..........it just means crying.

Anne..."Oh Shelley, Caroline she was so upset about not seeing you and was skating down the phone"! Weeeeeeee.

I mean, you'd pay to see that wouldn't you.

Would you like me to tell you about Caroline's claim to fame? Oh go on then.

Way back in the day before ice skating became rock 'n' roll (see how I did a cheeky link there) it was New Year's Eve and I together with Caroline and a bunch of other friend type persons were out on the town in Nottingham, it was New Year's Eve. Everyone was in a happy celebratory mood, including Caroline. She decided to take it a stage further however and as the chimes of the clock at the council building in the Market Square struck midnight she took it upon herself to celebrate by jumping into the fountains, yep, true as I'm sitting here typing. A rather handsome 'bobby' (policeman) along with a colleague strolled over to Caroline as she splashed about like a good 'un and said,

"Excuse me madam, would you mind getting out of the fountain, we know its New Year's Eve, but it's not very lady like".

She's not a bad girl, so getting out drenched and chuckling she asked,

"I've very sorry, are you going to arrest me"?

"No not this time, Happy New Year, now go and get yourself dry" said the blonde policeman shaking his head.

The gent in question was only Christopher Dean, yes, he of Torville and Dean, of 'the' Torville and Dean ice skating duo extraordinaire.

You see we were in Nottingham city centre and it was back when he pounded the streets as a policeman. I like to think that Caroline in some small way pushed him to give up policing (as that would have been his last festive season in uniform) and concentrate on ice dancing as a professional career as she waded about in the fountains and he thought to himself "Oh dear have you seen this, maybe I should take up ice skating full time". ☺

Now then, here's a twist in the tale, not so long after this, there were the dynamic duo getting a perfect six score across the board at the Olympics, so on returning home they do a lap of honour on an open top bus around Nottingham city centre.

I took my Mum there as she loved T & D. The Market Square was absolutely packed with people so proud of our home grown champions, all very eager to celebrate, flags were waved and children were up on 'Dad's shoulders as the open top bus circled the city. Many cheered, waving and throwing streamers, flowers, and some............jumped into the fountains! Look, if it's good enough for Londoners in Trafalgar Square then.......

What else can I tell you about Caroline? No, it's alright, our Caz won't mind. Ah yes, very early 80's and she decided to go to the Army recruitment place in town and ask where should she write to in order to get a couple of pen-pal's. Nice enough request don't you think. The chap at the desk gave her an address to write to and that same day she put pen to paper. You see, would this have the same ring if I'd have said "she tapped fingers to email".........no, it wouldn't. Two weeks later she phoned me almost delirious down the phone.

"Oh good grief, you should see what I'm looking at right now". Well I had no time to be guessing so I just asked "what"?

"Over two thousand replies. That's what"! And she continued to explain that over the past two days the postman had been knocking on the door and just handing over pile after pile of mail for her.

"Oh I can't believe it" she said "I don't know where to start". Anyhow we had the solution within the same week, My Mum and I went over to Caroline's home one evening so that I together with Caroline and the Mum's could sort out all the letters into 'The Good, The Bad and The Lovely'. Yes, a sherry or two was also consumed and I still remember it as being one of the most enjoyable nights 'in' that I've ever had. The good news is two fold, she did write to a few of the boys and developed friendships!..........And the postman never sued for injury at work.

Do you believe in divine intervention? You might do after reading this.

The Thursday for my meet with Anne arrived, 12noon on the steps of the Theatre Royal main doors. I arrived with a few minutes to spare. At ten past, there was no sign of Anne so I figured she must have missed her bus. Deciding not to move too far from that area I just walked up and down outside the main

entrance of the theatre, and looked in the windows of the doors just in case she'd decided to go and wait inside. As I peered in, there was a woman in the foyer who kept glancing over at me. For five to ten minutes we kept glancing over at each other. When all of a sudden with my back to the doors, I heard the door closest to me squeak open and a very enthusiastic voice said,
"Hi there, I'm so sorry, have you been waiting long"?
"Not really"? I said a little confused.
"Well come on in, she won't be long" said the woman.
So in I went. Don't really know what I was thinking, but we'd (Anne, Caroline) met at the theatre royal bar for lunch before so...........
"Would you like to come this way" said the woman and she guided me through the bar and into the Royal Concert Hall building.
I don't know why I didn't ask why we were going into the concert hall. She just seemed very organized and knew what was happening, so I just went along with it. The woman chatted ten to the dozen and was very forthright, so I didn't bother to question her. I was taken to a room where there were sandwiches and tea and coffee.
'Oh this is nice' I thought, nice room, quite civilized.
"Just help yourself my love, I'll be back with her in a while, she'll be here any minute, the others should be here soon", and off she trotted.
'I wonder how this woman knows Anne', I thought. I was confused however as to why I'd been brought to this room, and who were these 'others'. It looked like there was enough tea and coffee there for 20 people. I decided to pour myself a coffee and walked over to the window which looked down into the stair well. From where I stood I could see 'the woman' in the foyer of the concert hall, three people had now joined her and she was pointing up the stairs. They too eventually came into the room.

They all seemed to know each other, and smiled over at me and said 'hello' and glanced over the drinks and sandwiches. This began to feel weird. I decided to ask one of the threesome who this woman was.

"Oh I think her names Leila" replied one of the young men.

"Does she work here"? I asked.

"No, she's come up from London for the auditions" he replied.

Auditions!...... Now this is where you should be able to hear the 'Twilight Zone' music if you put your ear close enough to the page (come on, admit it, you did hold the book up to your ear just then didn't you!?). After further chat and investigation it appears the touring show I'd sent my CV in for (the 40's show I was rejected for due to my ageing bones!) was THIS...........this audition!

You might think to yourself 'well it was just a coincidence'. I could also go along with that had I not sent my CV to an address in Manchester!.....I know.........did you just get goosebumps? Immediately after this information being relayed to me, several other people entered the room followed by Leila who walked through the door accompanied by another rather striking looking woman with short red hair, as in RED hair.

"Hello everyone, thanks for waiting, sorry I'm late, damn train" she said waving her arms about. "So did you all get a tea? coffee? Ok, so I just need to make a call, everyone (she ushered with hand gestures) get a drink, eat the sandwiches, it's all paid for, I'll be ten minutes" and with that she was off out of the room again.

'Oh my goodness' I thought, 'somehow, I'm in the audition room for the show I was told I'm too old for........and how come it's here in Nottingham...........I couldn't think fast enough. What do I do now, what do I do'?

First things first I needed to find Anne.

I walked over to Leila,

"Leila, h-e-l-l-o 'erm would it be ok for me to just nip to the loo"
I asked.
"Of course, Sam will be at least 10 minutes, what's your name
again"? She said, looking down at her list.
'Oh well, this is where it's all going to go pear shaped' I thought.
"Shelley......James"? I said.
"Er, let me see, Shelley, Shelley" she said out loud looking down
at a folder..........umm don't seem to have you on the list Shelley,
but that's ok, we've had a girl cancel today so it's not a problem,
we do have a space" (*do do do do do do do dooo Twilight Zone
theme plays again*)
I then casually walked out of the room, and hurried down the
stairs and through to the bar then the foyer looking for Anne.
Sure enough she was there waiting on the steps.
"Mum! Mum! I called, you won't believe what's happened" and I
quickly filled her as fast as I could speak while dragging her into
the theatre bar, on the past 20 minutes of confusing drama.
"Oh you must go back, go back" Anne insisted.
"Yes I will, you wait here, I shouldn't be that long, I'm sure I'll
get found out before long" I laughed.
"Go, go, I be OK here" she said.
So I left Anne in the theatre's bar with a cuppa and biscuits to
keep her company.
As I arrived back in the audition room Sam had also just walked
back in and clapping hands for attention we all gathered around
for her pep talk.
"OK guys, there are fourteen of you, we just need six for the
tour, now then don't be disheartened, we have a another tour
going out in four months' time so if we can't use you now, chances
are we may be able to later in the year. Obviously there are
going to be disappointments today, but I want to thank you now
for all traveling here today, sorry about the confusion and hope

the last minute changes yesterday didn't cause any of you too much hassle".

Nope........it was no hassle at all for me!

We then did some warm up's and sang a song in unison, there were some great voices around me, and everyone was eager to impress for the six month contract. The rest of the audition for me was a bit of a blur. We sang another song and then Leila taught us a cheeky little dance number. I was half way through this number for the second time and then it happened. I went rather light headed and ended up in a heap on the floor. I'd had no breakfast, or lunch! And I think that together with the exertion of the dancing it just led to my light headed episode.

I remember lots of little faces looking over me, which was quite a shock initially as I don't remember 'landing' on the floor.

Leila and Sam fussed over me in a slight panic.

"Oh dear, are you OK" I could hear them saying as I lay there on the floor.

"I'm good" I replied "I just really like this carpet and wanted a closer look".

They, together with the others, laughed and helped me up to a nearby chair.

"Sit there a while" said Sam with a reassuring hand on my shoulder. Leila rushed back over to me with a glass of water.

"No need for you to do the rest of the routine Shelley" said Sam, we've almost finished anyhow, just sit there until you feel OK".

Around ten minutes later they were winding up the audition and we, the group, clapped in appreciation of being seen.

"Thank you for your time everyone" Leila called out "we will be in touch with you all regardless of the outcome in the next 7 days, safe journey home".

Sam and Leila were shuffling papers and photographs and as they did this one by one the lads and lasses that had been singing their hearts out, and dancing around the room together gathered their belongings and filed out of the room. I stood and began to put my jacket on when Sam walked over to me,

"How you feeling"? She enquired.

"I'm fine now, sorry about that, I feel so embarrassed" I said

"Oh no need to apologize, just glad you're OK, and while I've got you here on your own could you just fill out one of these", she said handing me an audition form, "it's just a formality so that we have your details, measurements and so on and I might as well tell you..............................we'd like you to do the tour". She said.

"Owww" I replied (resembling an owl, as in wide eyed with a pathetic look of surprise)

"Is that a good 'oww' or a bad 'oww'"? She queried looking surprised herself.

"It's a good 'oww', thank you so much" I said.

"I have to admit though (not letting out my secret) I didn't complete the whole audition and I think I may be a bit older than the others".

"Yeh, well that really isn't a problem as far as I'm concerned, I doubt you're older than me and I 'know' I'd still be capable of doing this tour. It may have been a problem if you'd have got Jude today, she was after the 20-28 age group for the show, but we didn't see eye to eye on that anyhow. She's in Manchester, she broke her ankle yesterday hence why I was sent here at the last minute, I'm working in Leicester tonight so it made sense for me to do the auditions here, but that aside, I can see something in you and I think you'd be a great addition to the group".

I loved that tour, very different to other work I've done, but fondly remembered.

Disappointment............. Followed by gleeful'ness.

Just like the end of a film........this time anyhow.

In my career I've had a lot of refusals at auditions too. Like, you're too tall, too short, too young, too old, too brunette, too blonde! Sorry there's only one of you we need two!!!

Time for a break... how's that coffee working out for you?

So audition refusals. Instantly I think of one in London where I was told at the door "Oh, didn't you know we're only looking at blondes"? No, no-one told me that, especially since I'd previously sent in a CV and a photograph, that 'they' replied to, of me with my brunette hair, bit of a give-a-way really. I decided the train fare shouldn't be in vain, so after the five minute stint of dropping into Pineapple dance studio and out again, I'd decided best plan of action was get a ticket to see a play. 'The Killing of Jessica' was the play of choice, not for any other reason than it was the cheapest price ticket! I'm just being honest. Bit of a shock when the maid turned out to be my friend Denise, so the trip to the capital not wasted as my day ended with a friends-reunited and meet with the cast.

Then there were the auditions that with some cheek I managed to land.
Great Yarmouth is the setting. As I arrived I knew that something was wrong, basically it was just me and eleven men. The chap holding the auditions said "Oh, we didn't really want a woman, Oh well you're here now". Again, my CV and photograph being a slight hint I was female. Everyone had to sing two songs, and do a spot of movement with a choreographer. At the end we were all asked why we'd be perfect for the job. The job in this particular case was a compare position. The boys were laying it on with a trowel...

"Well Stuart, I feel I can really bring something to the venue, I'm great with people, I'm also great at reading an audience, and although I say so myself, I excel in a crisis".

The next chap had his say...

"Stuart, my experience, if I may say so is second to none, I've worked with some of the biggest names in the business and had I not just had time off due to a medical emergency then I would be cruising with Tom O'Connor right now".

Ladies first? Not on your Nelly, all the boys had their say until the agent finally got to me............He asked.

"So Shelley, why do you think you'd be ideal for the position" I answered. "......because I'm not them?"

A bit cheeky, but they did go on............and on..........................and on. It paid off. I was offered the contract the following day.

It was one of two auditions that I've secured with just a few words. The second was an audition at Blackpool.

I have never in all my days seen so many people after so few contracts. It all began at 9.30am, and it was never ending.

"Ohhh hi there, I'm Veronica, and I'd like to sing for you bla bla bla" (I do hope there isn't a song out there called Bla Bla Bla, apologies if there is), and that's how the day ran out. Preened and pruned the glossy people would jump up onto the stage one by one announcing who they were and singing their choice of song, sometimes to be stopped half way through (which was often accompanied with tears) or allowing the wannabes to carry on through until the end of their song.

By 4pm I 'still' hadn't been seen. The 'judges' had secured three breaks to have a drink and freshen up, which was jolly nice for them, the rest of us were dropping like flies. I was eventually seen at 7.42pm (quite precise, but after 6pm every minute seemed like an hour)........I got up onto the stage, stood looking into the spot light and when the voice from behind the table called "Yes, and you are"?

"Hello" I answered "I've been here that long I've forgotten what my b........y name is".

There was a silence, and then laughter. I waited for the pianist to start but a woman walked over to him got hold of my music and walked over towards me.

'Oh well, never mind', I thought 'you can't win 'em all'. At this point I'd given up hope anyhow and just wanted to get back on the train and home.

She walked over to me, beckoned me from the stage and said "we have your details we'll be in touch, very brave, brilliant".

They did have my details and they did get in touch, sending me a 24 week contract. Eh hee, turned out nice again.

Ahh now then, let me tell you about a musician friend of mine who back in the day was reading through the Stage Newspaper (paper for the showbiz types, advertising, promoting shows, interviews, job vacancies etc) and whilst glancing over the job's/auditions available.........he noticed..........HIS OWN JOB!

He was a resident musician and couldn't believe his eyes. He hadn't been approached by anyone saying they didn't like his work or his personality. There had been, to his knowledge no complaints, nothing. Yet there it sat on the back pages of the paper, his own job, advertised as bold as brass. He wanted to find out what was going on, so phoned the number advertised and pretended to be 'Graham Foster' (This being a fictitious name and not to be associated with anyone living or otherwise of the same name). It was explained to 'Graham' that the position would be available in a month's time if he'd like to audition. How awful was that!

He sent in a bogus CV, used a friends address, and soon after sending this he was sent audition details. Now this was the tricky thing, he couldn't audition could he? It was 'his' job. So he contacted them and said how it was difficult for him as he was working on a tour so could he send a disc with some of his musical attributes on. They allowed this........he sent in a recording.........and a few days later, they contacted him, offering him the job............I mean............they offered him, his own job! It was all far too much for my head to process back then, and still rattles me now. He accepted it, HA, thinking it would give him some breathing space to decide what to do next. However a few days before he 'should' have started his own job he phoned the guy he'd been in contact with and said how he'd had a re-think, thanked them for their time but turned down the job. In all that time, no management or anyone approached my friend at the venue where he worked, and nothing was EVER mentioned, crazy.

The outcome............he kept his job. That evening I watched him on stage and he had this smug little look on his face. And why not, he'd beaten them at their own game, but how strange was all that?

Disappointment, this time followed by smugness (*puts coffee down.....goes over to dictionary.......trots back to coffee rather smugly*)....Arhhh smug'ness.......it's real, yep a real and proper-like word. *People cheer for miles around*.

Smugly?.................Smugglly?..............was that a character on the Banana Splits?

Interval over..

Meanwhile back in Nottingham. As I walked back to the theatres' bar to meet Anne, who at this point had consumed several cups of tea, well, I had the biggest smile on my face.

144

"Oh Shelley you back" she said in her lovely accent "You smile, ohhh you get yob"?

"Yes, indeed" I said "I got the yob, now come on lets get some lunch and I'll tell you about it".

I like to think of that day as a 'lucky break'! Well for me it was anyhow.

What would you say has been a turn of fate, a lucky break perhaps in your life?

Favourite overheard quote of the time.......

"....I don't know if I'm really flushed or I've just got too much blusher on."

Chapter Eleven... Food Glorious Food

It's only been in more recent years that I've discovered the ability to say, "er, no actually I can't do that" or "no thank you". Before this milestone I would just say yes to most things....mainly out of fear of not wanting to offend or upset. It would go something like this, "Shelley, can you just post this for me", Me "Yes", and "Oh would you mind picking up some dry cleaning in town", Me "Yes", oh and could you just do some dry stone walling".......................I would put myself into all matter of stressful situations, just so that I didn't upset people! Many times I was fine with any requests, if I could do them I would, but there were the occasions where I knew as the words came out of my mouth "Yes I will", I knew I should've been saying "Sorry, no I can't". This need to please also went into foodstuffs. And I think my Mum's constant battle with me as a child when at the table "eat ya greens there's a good girl, they'll do you good" had an adverse effect on me. It didn't work. Even though I tried for many years I've never liked cabbage, cauliflower or Brussels sprouts, uuh. Despite trying them over and over again, they have never pleased my taste buds. But that constant need to please people means I've sat and eaten all of the above if it's been cooked for me, in the distant past I've even eaten coffee cake, tripe and onions and blue cheese! Oh I feel ill just thinking about it all. But not lamb.....That is where I drew the line along time ago, not since the age of 6/7 when it actually clicked what lamb was...........it was.........lamb.......no, no, don't let's go any further.......trust me, there 'will' be tears.

So taking all of that into account and we go back to the noughties! There I was in Nottingham doing a little lunch time cabaret spot for an 'older anniversary couple'. It was a lovely gentle party and a fine time was had by all. Stuff all packed away in the car afterwards and the jobs a good'un. Before returning home it was decided beforehand 'we' (husband Alan and myself) would nip and see my step Mother Teresa. She only lived a hop, skip and jump away so it seemed silly not to pop in for an hour or so and have a cuppa. As predicted she was delighted to see us on this little unexpected visit, and no sooner we were through the door the kettle was on. I explained the reason I had hair extensions in trimmed with diamante and full stage make-up on, was that I'd just done a show up the road. "Did they feed you"? She asked.

"Er no" I said, "but it's ok because..........."

But I got no further with the explanation as she hurried into the kitchen and the clatter of pots and pans filtered through to the dining room where we sat. She hobbled back into the room like a bossy waitress. "Right, what can I get you, you want pie? I have pie"? We both leaned forward in a strange body language way to appear more forceful with our replies of "Oh no, no, we're fine, you don't need to go to any trouble". But she ignored us, spoke louder and just kept asking us about pie and then went into a whole menu of things she had that we could eat. It got embarrassing, and 'he' Alan that is then began to get that nervous laugh you adopt when you don't know how to handle a situation and looked across at me as if to say "well come on, say something that will solve this". It was like a battle and the generous polish lady was not going to give in without a fight. "You MUST eat, EAT" she demanded. There was not going to be any winning in this battle, well, not for us anyhow.

So I gave in and said "well alright, but just something simple". "Ok, simple, ok" said Teresa, "well omelette, yes, you eat omelette"?

I'd actually meant a sandwich, but I don't think something 'that' simple would have pleased her, so as we'd obviously been defeated I said "ok, an omelette". She then went back into the kitchen and the noises of a well run café could be heard in the distance.

"I'm not that hungry" said Alan,

"tough, you've got to eat it, it'll be alright" I said.

Famous last words. Teresa appeared at the door,

"Tea, you want more tea"? She asked. We both nodded and I said how I'd prefer a coffee. "Tea for Alan and coffee for you, are you starving, you must be starving, I make omelette, terrible to not feed you, you eat soon, you 'will' be hungry"? She continued. I s'pose it was possible, but we'd had breakfast several hours previous so it was highly unlikely we were 'actually' starving!

More tea and coffee arrived and as she popped in and out of the dining room with chat I could smell the aroma of eggs, mushrooms, cheese and..............ummm, cant detect what that other smell is....but not to worry, it's an omelette, what could possibly go wrong.

A little later she arrived in the room with a tea towel over one arm and a plate filled to extreme with a large omelette in the other hand, in fact the biggest omelette you ever did see (and now why am I thinking 'that sounds like a Tommy Steel song'?). Where food was involved Teresa didn't skimp. "Alan, sit, sit, sit, come on" and ordered Alan to get to the table and eat. "I make yours now (looking over at me) and I make drinks". And with that she was off again into the kitchen to make an omelette for myself and even more drinks. Alan looked at his omelette like it was going to bite him.

"What's up"? I said.

"Oh nooooo, it's not right this, it's not right, look", and he lifted the omelette to reveal the underside looking decidedly wet, undercooked, weirdly crumbly and with a strange mix of the previous mornings breakfast! And the top was like a hard hat with a black trim.

"Oh no, no, I can't eat this" he said near to tears..............drama queen.

"You have to, she's made it 'specially for us" I said like a ventriloquist.

"I can't, I just can't" he said loudly whispering 'at' me, and up he stood picking up the plate and heading towards the door.

"What are you doing, where you going with that" I said, still in ventriloquist guise.

"I've got to get rid of it" he said.

"What!! NO, you can't, it will upset her, no, noooooooo". I'd now spoken for so long without moving my lips it felt like I'd got lock jaw.

"Well I can't eat it, look at it, I just can't, I can-not eat this" and off towards the door he strode again.

"What are you doing"? I said "You can't tell her, she'll be devastated".

"I'm not" he replied "I'm going to put it down the loo".

Teresa's house had a small downstairs toilet across the hall from the dining room, and Alan was off.......I chased after him.

"Stop, stop it" I quietly yelled!!!!

"No, I've got to get rid of it" he said, plate out in front of him like an unexploded bomb!

"Will you stop it" I said "you can't put it down there, what if it doesn't flush".

"I'll have to take that chance" he said.

I just couldn't risk that happening so I grabbed hold of the other side of the plate and we then did the push me, pull me dance! It was like a Brian Rix farce. "No you can't". "Yes, I can" being the lyrics to the dance! After a short blast of push me, pull me time we heard Teresa call "Alan, two sugars yes"? We both scuttled back into the dining room, omelette intact.

"Yes, two sugars love" he called back and then looked at me with a Wallace and Gromit grimmice.

"Oh give it here" I said, and without hesitation he thrust the plate at me and sat down at the table. One of the reasons I thought it might be a good idea to pop to Teresa's in the first place was my step sister Maria's birthday was looming the following week and I'd got her a lovely but very breakable gift, so was weary about posting and it arriving in a thousand pieces. So the night previously I'd wrapped it in tissue paper, then bubble wrap, popped it into a box, wrapped up the box in pretty paper and then the final touch put the pretty box into an even prettier sparkly gift bag. The gift bag since arriving with us had sat on the floor at the side of the couch. I lifted the box out of the bag quickly chucked the omelette into the sparkly bag, rushed back over to Alan and placed the now empty plate in front of him 'just' as Teresa came back into the room with drinks……phew.

"Oh, you eat Alan, very fast, good, good, you hungry" she said.

"Yeh, that's enough though Teresa couldn't eat another thing, thank you" he said.

"Oh no, I have cake, you eat a cake, yes, eat some cake" and before we knew it she'd done a return trip to the kitchen and come back in with some of Mr. Kiplings finest. I sat with my coffee gently tapping the gift bag further back with my foot and then lay my jacket over the arm of the sofa to disguise its presence…..or present….s! Soon she was back in the dining room with another spectacular omelette, this one was for me.

"Ohhh, look at thiiiiisss" I said, I was apprehensive, worried and all other words that come with panic. Did I get the support I'd shown Alan?

Of course I didn't.

As Teresa sat directly opposite me at the table smoking and drinking her tea, Alan sat there with his fondant fancy grinning from ear to ear. How on earth was I expected to eat this? It had arrived with all the same charm as the previous serving, but the problem was, with Teresa planted firmly in the room and a smarmy husband at the table, how was I going to get rid of this one. We all chattered and I cut through (eventually) the rubber like omelette. With a piece of it on my fork, as it got closer to my mouth, I kept thinking, 'you can do this, it's really chocolate, it's really chocolate' (a mantra I'd used for many years as a kid when faced with vegetable nasties). 'Voila', it was in my mouth…………………………oh good grief……………………………. uuhhhhh……..this was not chocolate by any stretch of the imagination……….what was that exactly? …….al la carte tyre?? I chewed and chewed and chewed as the two of them chatted about this n' that. No one was moving………. I mean, no one……I looked across at himself with wide eyes and 'HELP ME' bubbles coming out of my head like a cartoon rabbit in the headlights. But nooooooo he sat there enjoying his tea and more cake. I proceeded with a second mouthful on the fork. At this point I need to advise you……..if you ever find yourself in this situation, there is a safe period where you can just put your knife and fork down, and chew, and not take a second mouthful, for, ohhhh quite some time. However, fifteen minutes is not advisable, things start to look suspicious. I was desperate. This did not taste good, but that aside, this lady would have given you her last penny, she was also quite a force of nature, food meant a great deal to her having been starved of it in terrible circumstances as a child, so I just couldn't say 'no'. Omelettes just weren't her thing, but I couldn't and wouldn't hurt her feelings, so I had to come up with a plan B.

I can't drink hot drinks as in 'HOT' drinks, and so as mine had just arrived and was indeed 'hot', I had to sacrifice the inside of my mouth to give me some breathing space. Alan just sat there a-gog as I guzzled down the mega hot drink, sweat pouring off me and my cheeks going a rather fetching shade of red.

"Ohhh, ohhh, quite 'er thirsty, yeh, very thirsty" I said shaking all over as id just subjected myself to the equivalent of hot lava.

"Could I be cheeky Teresa" I said "don't suppose I could grab another coffee could I"?

"Yes, yes, you can", and off she went again kitchen bound. As she left the room Alan was demanding to know why I'd been so stupid to drink such a hot drink. I dived over to the sparkly bag, whipped it up to the table and scooped two thirds of my omelette in to it. "Oh and the rest and the rest" Alan encouraged.

My ventriloquist routine now in full swing "don't be stupid" I said "If I do that, chances are she'll just go and make another".

"Ohhh riiighhht" he replied, 'clink' (that was the penny dropping). I placed the bag back down at the side of the sofa. Made sure the jacket was draped over the arm and jumped back onto my seat at the table with just under half the 'eaten' omelette in front of me. It was starting to get silly!!!

Teresa came back into the room. "Coffee for Shelley" she announced.

"Thanking you" I said.

"Oh, no, you not eat your omelette" she said. "Er, no" I replied "bit full, but thank you anyway". There was a pause, it went quiet. I looked at Alan, Alan looked at me, and then Teresa said, ".....so this couple you sing for today, what was it again, birthday? anniversary"?.............. YES! The omelette drama was done, it was over, I could hear birds singing again..............well, it was almost done. We still had the problem of ninety five percent of it still sitting in a sparkly bag in Teresa's dining room at the side of the sofa.

Another hour went by, and to keep up the pretence of dire thirst another two coffees were consumed. After this less fraught hour went by, there also began something we hadn't bargained for, the aroma of stale omelette wafting around the room from the floor. "Oh Alan" I said "er can you nip to the car and get Maria's gift, it's behind the seat". As quick as you like he replied "Oh, I thought you brought it in with you"... (I give up)................"NOOOO" I said "I didn't.....YOU NEED to go and get iittttt, noowwww". At this point I was in the frame of mind of 'where can I get some quick 10 by 8's done to promote my new vent act'.

'Clink' (that was the penny dropping for the second time) "Owwwww riiiiightttt" he said, and I gestured with a sideways nod towards the sparkly bag.

I quickly threw myself onto the sofa and picking up my jacket and the bag underneath I passed them to himself stating in a higher pitched voice and of amateur dramatics style......

"Oh and take this jacket toooo, I don't think I'll be neeeeeding it anymore today, please leave it in the car wont yooouuu".

And wonders with never cease.......he actually twigged on and took the sparkly bag and my jacket out to the car.

While this happened as a decoy to Alan's exit I wildly (and I mean seriously over the top like she'd won a car in some fabulous competition) and excitedly announced "Ohhh Ohhhhh oh silly me, ooohhh here, here is Maria's Birthday gift, I did bring it in after all" and I presented the prettily wrapped box like it was gold, frankincense or myrrh.

Coming back in from the car Alan gave me the thumbs up sign..........subtle! We stayed approximately another 15 minutes and then decided it was probably time to go.

We thanked Teresa for feeding and watering us and said how we'd visit again soon, to give Maria our love and how we hoped she'd have a lovely birthday. We walked down the path, out of the gate opened the car door and 'eewwooowwweeeee'.....what a stench! The omelette was well and truly fermenting!

On getting inside the car, Teresa then insisted on telling us some belated news whilst standing at the car door. 'Oh hurry up' I was thinking while the rotting omelette released its toxic fumes within the car. Eventually she came to the end of her story, and the funniest part was, she never did end it in full, as she forgot the punch line and the reason for telling us in the first place! Oh well. As we started the car and moved away from the house waving like lunatics, (A, to wave 'ta-ta' and B, to waft the smell around a bit) we saw Teresa go back into the house and Alan pulled up at the end of the road.

"What are you doing"? I asked.

"I'm going to put the omelette into that waste bin there" he said pointing at a waste bin outside of the post office.

"You can't do that" I demanded. "What happens if she nips out to the shops tomorrow and just happens to see a beautiful sparkly bag in a waste bin, knowing Teresa she would want to rescue it and take it home, noooooo".

He said "well I hardly think it's going to be in a police line up of omelettes".

"No" I insisted, "we can't do that, it would be just our luck to get caught out in some fashion and then I'd feel even worse than just saying "I can't eat this Teresa". No, we have to take it further away. So we did. With the car windows right down due to the now suffocating smell and me sticking my head out of the window like an Afghan Hound on its way to the seaside, oh, we took it further away alright, seven miles away to a place called Tythe Green Burial Ground. No, we didn't bury it.......maybe we should have. Once there we pulled into the car park where there was indeed a waste bin………..opened all the doors to the car to 'give it a good blow through', and then placed sparkly bag with its contents into the waste bin. I got some strange looks from a couple obviously on their way to pay respects to a loved one. There I am, hair all bouffant'ed, diamante'd up to within an inch of my life, full stage make up, placing a very sparkly bag into the waste bin. Actually if you say that fast enough it doesn't sound so weird! Oh how we look back and laugh now……No…..sorry, not laugh, cringe, how we look back and cringe now!

I'd like to think in the big scheme of things we gave that poor old omelette a rather dignified end. It was quite a day due to my inability to refuse people.

But in future kids, just remember what the motto was at the fictitious school of Grange Hill on the tele………Just Say No!

That's all for now……..more later. It's just that I must go, I've got something on a low light.

Have you ever been in a situation that has got completely out of hand due to your good manners?

Favourite overheard quote of the time…….

"…….I just can't move fast in these slippers. I don't know why I got them really. I've got an identical pair upstairs."

Chapter Twelve... Papa Can You Hear Me

One of my all-time favourite summer seasons was at Osmington Bay in Weymouth. I'm calling it a Summer Season, but with it starting in April and finishing at the end of October it would be more appropriate to call it 'that time I moved down south'.
I was a bluecoat and shared my season with some smashing people who became friends, Paula, Avon, David, Carol, Robin, Christine, Jan, Colin.....and anyone else that knows me ☺ (not really but I've always wanted to say that!)
We worked hard, heck did we work hard, and we would retire to our little sheds at the end of each working day, sometimes to just crash onto the bed and drift off fully clothed into the land of nod, until the alarm clock would ring the following morning. Then the times when the duties had ended for the day and we'd dash back to 'the sheds' to quickly get changed and hit the towns' nightclubs. Oh to be young and reckless again, or perhaps, oh to be young again!
All too often we would finish work, get changed, go back into the ballroom and rehearse until the early hours for on-going or future production shows. Whilst rehearsing for one particular show Peter Linden, our show director, decided that when David and I sang 'Slow Boat to China' as a duet, it would be nice staging if we didn't come on from the back of the stage, but from a side staircase that led onto the ballroom dance floor. It seemed a rather strange idea, but we went along with it. Trouble is, there was only one way we could do this, so out of the fire door at the back of the dressing room area we would go, around the back of the building, into the fire doors at the side of the bar, through the bar, down the steps and there we were, on the ballroom floor, why have a simple option when you can make it as complicated as possible!

The show night would arrive each week and each time as Paula was singing her song, David and I would go out through the fire door, around the back of the building, and make our way in through the fire doors and through the bar, down the stairs, Paula would slink off the stage and there, often to the surprise of the spotlight operator, David and I would be crooning............"I'd like to get you, on a slow boat to China.................." Peter had a good eye for staging and it did look impressive actually.

One particular week it didn't quite happen the way we'd rehearsed. I finished my dance with Avon, dashed through to the changing area, got changed into my 'China' costume, David rushed through to meet me, we darted out of the fire door and it was pouring with rain, however we couldn't turn back as the fire door had already closed behind us, so we rushed around to the bar, where, due to the weather possibly being awful, the fire door there hadn't been opened for us. We rushed back hoping 'someone' may have re-opened the door, which they hadn't. We stood banging on the door, but figuring everyone must be busy getting changed off we ran again back to the door of the bar ....and the rain came down, real serious hard fat rain, you know the sort that gets you soaked. We both stood there like drowned rats knocking on the door, but due to the band no one could hear us. Paula's song, 'When Irish Eye's Are Smiling', was getting closer to the end and we were nowhere near the staircase to do our big entrance. The pair of us stood getting drenched with radio mics in hand, and we could hear our music starting.

"Shall we just sing and hope it picks us up" asked David

"That's all we can do" I said.

So yes, as our music reached our cue we began to sing the song..........."I'd like to get you, on a slow boat to China, all to myself alone.........." And as the song went on we could see people

157

looking around as if to say 'we can hear the voices, but we have no idea where their coming from'. Eventually one of the bar staff noticed us and rushing over opened the door to let us in. Just as the song was finishing we made it down onto the dance floor looking like we'd just fallen out of the slow boat into the ocean en route to China. The audience roared with approval. To this day I'm sure the audience that particular week thought our soaked entrance was all part of the show. I had to laugh, getting backstage after the song and Paula saying "Oww what's happened"? With David quipping "Oh nothing, we always look like this when we do our duet, haven't you ever noticed before".

Avon and I once took a group of 20 guests on a ramble over the cliffs to a nearby local pub. For some odd reason we'd gone in fancy dress?! That aside it was a lovely day, not too hot and not too cold (I sound like Goldilocks). With beautiful scenic views it was always a pleasure to be on that duty. The guests were such great company and the walk there was so entertaining and fun. People certainly make a place. As a rule we (whoever was on the ramble) would sit outside with a soft drink on reaching the pub and an hour or so later, we'd all have a nice stroll back. This particular day we were invited into the pub by our guests and drinks were constantly bought for us. I got a sing-song going and the whole bar joined in. It was a great atmosphere. The thing is, I remember getting there, but not getting back, apart from a mini-bus turning up and we all loaded onto it, as both we and the guests were blathered. How very unprofessional. Good ramble though!

Anyone reading who have had the pleasure of doing a season as a 'coat' will know only too well the relationships you'd build up with guests, whether you want to or not in some cases. I think every single week someone would say to me in passing "Oh you really remind us of our grand-daughter/daughter/neice, we'll bring a photograph in tomorrow and show you". These photos never resembled you, other than sometimes the culprit had a similar jumper on! So often you'd have a photograph thrust in front of you where the 'grand-daughter' had sticky out ears and a five o'clock shadow, 'ahhhh lovely'. Yes, it became an art in knowing what to say so that you didn't offend,

"Owww, well will you look at her", and "So that's her, mmmmm", being two of my standard replies.

Sometimes if you happened to be off guard then, oh dear. Without giving away the name, one of my friends and fellow 'coat' was sitting in a huddle of guests once and they were proudly showing off photos of their grandkids,

"Oh he's a bonny little chap" said Carol (oops, sorry Carol) as she was passed photo after photo to coo over.

"That's our grand-daughter Abigail" said the grandmother sternly, and all other photos were gathered up in silence as Carol made a discrete exit.

Then there's the time where you've sat chatting to a couple 20 minutes or more and you find yourself saying,

"So, have you been here before"?

There's an awkward silence, no one is filling in any of the quiet gaps, so you smile nervously only to be informed,

"Er, we've been writing to each other for the past 5 months, surely you recognize us?"

You go hot, a little bit pins and needles and you feel like there's no way out of this awkward situation, then you have a brain wave. Did they ever fall for the reasoning of............

"Oh yesssss, I knowwww we have, I meant, tooooooo 'this' particular bar (looks around room as if the bar was built in the

afternoon of that very day)...I thought we met in the ballroom..........nooooo"?
Listen in the world of entertainment, you're lucky if you sleep once during a season, things can and do get a little muddled as to whom you've met before and who you haven't.

Early pantomime days now and the dressing rooms at this venue were underneath the stage. This was fine, unless there was an over excitable dance routine in full swing and it sounded like a herd of elephants jumping up and down on your head. Or you had the giggles with a fellow cast member in the dressing room (it does happen) and there was a gentle ballad happening a few feet above you, then you had to stifle any giggles.
Unfortunately this pantomime season was marred with a light fingered singleton taking what didn't rightly belong to him or her. So not only did we have extra fast costume changes to contend with and dashing in and out of the dressing room, we also had to make sure the last person out also locked the door behind them. Our prompt lady that season being renamed 'key lady', due to her having kindly volunteered duty of looking after dressing room keys whenever the stage was full of 'cast'.
Yes it did dampen the spirits a little, but, the show must go on.....where have I heard that before? So without fail each time the dressing room was empty, last one out locked up.
I was in the chorus and as a singer, dancer, I shared the dressing room with 7 others, t'was busy.
We had mirrors and dressing tables all around the room and a big hefty rail that hung from the ceiling in the centre of the room which was home to all the costumes. The theatre was old and so often the lights from the stage would peep through the old worn wooden floor boards above our heads. Our prince that season

Rachel, had a few days of being full of cold and as she sang her duet with the princess one evening we all sat quietly in the dressing room looking up at the ceiling-'dash'-floor boards willing our friend to get through the song without her voice giving up on her. 'She made it', she sang the song and didn't falter once.......so we all cheered.

Moments later she was knocking on our dressing room door and pushing it open saying "Hello you lot, I got through it, thank you for the support, I could hear you all ya know".

That same weekend, I think most of the cast had picked up some sort of cold. The juves always ready to oblige in sharing their coughs and colds ☹ but with four shows to do over two days it was going to be a struggle.

Our dressing room which as a rule would smell of perfumed body sprays and various scents in the air, now whiffed like the back door of a chemist. Lotions and potions were shared about, as opposed to the usual Christmas sweeties. I hadn't lost my voice but I like many others in the cast had a head cold, as in, the letter 'D' came before most things.

D'costumes, D'audience and quite appropriately D'dancing.

The big number just before the interval was approaching and we were all changing into our costumes. The coughing and spluttering exceeded any cheery chat we usually had to offer. My nose just wouldn't stop running and I was anxious that this would perhaps hinder me on stage. Just as all the girls were running out of the dressing room for the number, I quickly turned back, raced around the clothes rail to my dressing table and picked up a tissue, 'better to have a tissue out there' I thought. I mean, in the olden times of Mother Goose surely ye people of the olde ye village had ye colds did they ye not.

I rushed back to the door and 'tug tug', I'd been locked in. 'Ow er, now what'.

Yes, I was in the chorus. Yes, 7 of the 8 of us were poised and ready in the wings to walk onto the stage.....and yes, I heard that happening above me. But, and this is a big but, so I'll emphasize it....BUT, I had a verse to sing in the song..........on my own, with no one with me, but me.

I knew there was no way out, no one would be back stage now either (apart from possibly our 'souvenir hoarder') so I panicked as to what I should do next. I looked up, the stage lights teasing me through the floor boards.

'Ow, I wonder'.......................... Quick as a flash I grabbed my chair. Stood on it, pressed the side of my face against the ceiling and waited for my cue. The music played tum-te-tum-te-tum..........I began............

"Once a 'd'onely caterpillar sat an' cried, to a d'impathetic creature by his d'ide....I've got nobody to d'ove, I'm just an ugly d'bug........" and so on.

I even joined in with the full chorus at the end.........Ohhh, no, no, honestly it was nothing. I was standing on the chair anyway!

When my chorus buddies returned to the dressing room, they were all laughing saying "we suddenly realized as the song began you weren't with us on the stage, 'n' that we must have accidentally locked you in"

"Yes, but could you hear me"? I asked.

"Yeeessss" came back the girls, (answering in the full chorus they'd been employed to be)

"But we couldn't quite figure out where your voice was coming from until we saw 'The Goose' looking down at the floor. He bent down and then knelt on the floor so that the mic around his neck could pick you up".

I've heard of stranger things happening. What am I saying, no, I haven't.

This show was sponsored by Vicks Synex.

There is a term used for entertainers/actors called 'resting'. It's a strange word to use really, as you'd think it means, holiday, or just relaxing at home. When for the likes of the entertainment world, it actually means, 'out of work'.

So now that's been explained, I can tell you I'd just finished a touring show and had 7 weeks before a pantomime was due to start so I was 'resting'....ummm.

I'd heard there was an agency in Nottingham that had been publicizing as they were on the lookout for Sing-O-Grams. Remember those? I phoned up and 48 hours later I was doing my first 'gig'. I'd better explain what they are/were, just in case you haven't heard of this before, or decided to forget about them. It was basically a male or female, dressing up in some form of costume, and singing Happy Birthday (as a rule, sometimes it was anniversaries) to someone unexpectedly. So you'd find yourself going to people's homes, parties, work places, in fact anywhere where the chosen Birthday girl or boy would be. My strangest venue engagement was on the platform of Nottingham Railway Station. Family and friends would 'set them up', so it was a little bit 'Surprise' coupled with a song. I learned very early on that if you personalized a song it would be to your advantage. While we would be paid by the agency, the tip from a recipient was often bigger. Listen, a girl's gotta eat......oh and buy pretties.

There I was, my first ever Sing-A-Gram customer, after singing Happy Birthday, and possibly due to fear of it being 'the first gig', I sang quite impromptu, (to the tune of New York, New York) "Start spreading the news, his party's today, he's gonna drink the bar at it, that's Mark that's Mark". And his guests all cheered in mass approval and a jolly time proceeded.

I think back to that time and my friend saying to me "Don't ya feel daft, walking into an office full of strangers in high heels, fishnet tights, top hat and tails" (and of course I wore things under that, it was all very classy). But no, not really, I didn't feel daft. Like an actor that is usually a mild mannered person that's suddenly given a role where he or she is the most evil person on the planet you just adopt a different persona. Let me explain it this way, had you have asked me to walk into an office full of people I didn't know in my regular day to day clothes and sing Happy Birthday to someone I'd never met. I'd have said, "no way". Slap on the make-up and costume and you're a different person. I did the job for a month and enjoyed it actually. The whole fad of the 'Sing-O-Gram', as well as the 'Strip-O-Gram' ('Oh I say' tut tut tut) seemed to be a wild craze that was hugely popular for a time and then disappeared over night, strange.

In my second week I was asked to go to a factory and sing for a chap celebrating his 50th Birthday. I arrived and at the reception, I announced who I was and what I was doing there, gave the receptionist the chaps details and the department he worked in and asked for directions. His workmates had set up the 'treat'. What was I saying about taking on a different persona? Distance walker may have been apt for this 'gig'. I had THE longest walk ever, and had to walk past so many people through this factory. As if it was the most natural thing in the world to be dressed in top hat and tails on a Tuesday afternoon. I'd just nod and carry on walking by saying "ya'alright".

'Smile gracefully Shelley, job will be done shortly and you'll soon be out of here' I kept telling myself.

I eventually reached my subject, the machine noise all died down and everything went quite as I announced the chaps name and everyone downed tools to watch their pal receive his birthday gift. I sang Happy Birthday, read out a saucy poem written by a work pal, and posed with the Birthday boy as one flash after another blinded me. Meaning camera's flashing, nothing sordid.

He was very sweet, and said his wife would kill him, but his mates all cheered and jeered with threats of blackmail if he didn't get the first round in at the pub after work, boys!!!

I stood and chatted and then after around 15 minutes the supervisor called 'Right then gents back to work'. There was still a vibe in the air of excitement due to the day's unusual interruption, I said my goodbyes and off I went.

I eventually made my way out of the huge noisy machine filled room and down a corridor. Then down another corridor, and then another, down a staircase, along another corridor, and another. Then I realized I'd gone a full circle and I was back at the room I'd just left. So a little embarrassed and not wanting anyone to see me, I trotted off with my head bent down in the opposite direction, where I basically wandered around owww, 20 minutes!

"Ask for directions ya nincompoop" I said to myself, but it wasn't so easy to do that.

Partly due to embarrassment, and also I could see lots of people at machines, noisy machines, but not many people I could just approach. I eventually found a sign that said 'Wages Office', and reaching there I said to some ladies,

"Hi, I seem to be lost, could you point me in the direction of the main doors please, I've been wandering around for about 20 minutes". It was cringingly embarrassing. No one broke a smile, just looked me up and down and then one lady stood up from her desk, sighed, walked out of the office, stared at me and huffed (what was wrong with her? never seen anyone in a top hat and tails before) walked behind me and pushed open a door within 2 feet of me leading outside saying, "Main door, just there".

In a strange blind panic I'd passed the main doors three times. Oww, I felt such a fool.

At the end of that same week I had three Sing-O-Gram dates to attend. The first being on the Saturday morning, the second one during Saturday afternoon, and finally one in the evening. I'd taken three on due to one of the girls being poorly and not being able to attend her booking that afternoon. It was quite a busy day.

In the evening I'd arranged to go out with my cousin Debbie. "Why don't I pick you up" she said, "then you can get changed at the venue where you're doing ya work, we can pop ya costume in the boot of the car and we can go out afterwards", great idea. The evening arrived and as arranged, together with cuz I walked into the hotel in the centre of Nottingham, spiky haired and coat tailed, versatile! Walked into a party room where I sang my head off to the Managing Director Birthday boy of a huge company. He and his wife were so kind towards Debbie and I. After I'd got myself changed into 'going out' clobber, they offered us drinks and food. We stayed a short while then made polite noises to excuse ourselves, said our 'ta-ta's' and off we went deciding to go and have a night out in a club just the other side of the River Trent. We got back into the car and headed down the main road through the city centre. There was a young man, a little the worse for wear, calling out at three girls as we sat in the traffic lights queue. You could tell from his body language he was being quite aggressive.

"What's his problem, what's he on about"? asked Deb.

"I don't know" I answered "but he's just upset those girls".

A couple of people approached him in an attempt to shut him up, but the little nuisance had just walked out of the Kentucky Fried Chicken take-a-way with a closed box of chicken snacks, waving his arms about and generally being very obnoxious, and any sort of reasoning just wasn't being acknowledged.

"Oh, he's at it again" said Deb "look, he's being horrible to those girls".

And as she said it the lights changed and the traffic queue began to gradually and slowly move forwards.

The irritant was now standing, waiting at the crossing, mouthing off and desperately trying to keep his balance. With his box of chicken proudly in front of him, he swayed and tilted and it had obviously been quite a good night out......not that he'd remember that the following day.

"I should just take that box from him as we pass him Debbie" I said, "teach him a lesson for being a pain".

"OH I DARE YA", said Debbie.

Well.............I didn't need to be dared twice, down came the passenger side window and as we became level with him moving along with the traffic I just swiped the box straight out of his hands, whilst calling in a very posh voice "Oh thank you so much" and I looked in the side mirror as we drove away to see him looking at his hands, the floor, even the sky, totally confused as to where his Kentucky Fried treat had evaporated to.

Never in our lifetime of being cousins, did Debbie and I laugh so much as we did that night.

We happened to see the city's 'resident tramp' further down the road, so pulled over and I passed him the meal. You know, I can see that man now. I don't think there was ever a time being a kid to young adult that I went into the city centre and didn't see that man. He looked like the image of Jesus. Long hair, long beard, but he was a big broad man. And I'm not being disrespectful calling him a tramp, 'he' was the one that would announce, 'I'm the city's resident tramp you know"! He was no trouble at all, always having a friendly hello for you. He could often be seen chatting to the police who knew him well. I would often see him while waiting for my friends in town, he'd casually be walking by in a long coat that I have no idea what its original colour was, but it resembled mucky brown. I used to think 'how on earth has it come to this for this man'. He was quite intelligent and I don't ever remember seeing him beg. People would just walk up to him and hand things to him like drinks, food, spare change etc.

Cuz Deb and I never did go to that club, I think in the hysteria we took a wrong turning and ended up at a bar called Tree Tops in totally the opposite direction.

Back home in the wee small hours, I was creeping up the stairs trying desperately not to wake anyone, when halfway up I heard my Mum,

"Have you had a good night duckie", she said whispering. I looked up and there was Mum sitting perched on the top of the stairs.

"Ohh yeh, sooooo funny" I said. "What are you doing there" I asked.

"Well its quite late n' I was worried" she said.

It wasn't late really, it was quite early, 3.15am in fact.

I sat down at the side of her and I relayed the story about how after the sing-a-gram the evening took an unexpected turn incorporating the tale of the noisy chicken man.

"Ow you shouldn't have done that"? She said whilst laughing.

"I know, but hopefully taught him to be respectful otherwise ya chicken goes missing" I said.

We both then sat huddled up together at the top of the stairs giggling like school girls.

A voice then came out of the darkness.

"To say you two are whispering, I know all about the bloke who's Birthday it wa', what our Debbie was wearing, how much a double is up'at Tree Tops and the poor bloke who had his chicken nicked............now shurrup the pair of ya"

I take it Dad could hear me then.

Do you recall Chinese whispers amounting to something it really didn't start off as, or have you overheard something you wish you hadn't?

Or was it you that had your chicken taken?

Favourite overheard quote of the time.

"*No I haven't taken any painkillers yet, I'm just waiting to see how bad it gets.*"

Chapter Thirteen... It's A Grand Night for Singing

The Grand Hotel once again is the setting for this next bunch of tales of the unexpected. This time we find ourselves in the early 1990's.

It wasn't the day some men wandered into the hotel stating they were there to repair the TVs from the whole of the first floor and then strolled out as cocky as you like with all the TV's...........Men and TV's never to be seen again!

And it wasn't the day four pensioners got stuck in the lift for just short of an hour, so we had to call the fire brigade. Turns out absolutely nothing wrong with the lift, only the fact the people in it kept pressing 'doors closed', instead of 'doors open'. Not a bad day though, I mean, we had to call out the fire brigade ☺

And no, it wasn't the day Wendy on reception called me over to show me what they'd found as lost property. A carrier bag, with a solitary item of a top set of dentures tucked inside, ewww. So many questions really! The main being, 'how do you leave the hotel with no top teeth in, and you don't notice'?

The thing that 'was' happening however was the hotel having some quite extensive refurbishments and so we shared the hotel on a daily basis for quite some time with a selection of builders and decorators. They were staying in the hotel so they would be around first thing until the end of each working day. At this time I was singer with the band and directing the shows. Each time we had a show, beforehand in the girl's dressing room there would be all the usual chat plus gossip about who's going out with whom, regarding staff and workmen! Grand Hotel meets 'Blind Date'! As the weeks went on, the same name kept cropping up..........let's say it was 'Dave' (as he's possibly a respectable married man now with children....protect the innocent and all that). Well 'Dave' had a bit of a reputation I'll have you know. I'll bet he'd never had a job like it.

Taking on the self-penned title of 'God's Gift' he was dating and flirting with most of the female staff in the building. His friends would egg him on, and he was also the butt of their jokes, but he seemed oblivious. Admitted he was a looker, and he used this to his advantage, but he was breaking hearts right, left and centre. A few of 'us girlies' in the entertainment department got our heads together and over some coffee meet ups, came up with a little plan in order for him to get his comeuppance. It happened over a few days as one by one we gradually flirted with him. We gave him a false sense of security and fawned over him like he was the only man on the planet. Of course with an ego the size of his he just believed every word, even though what was actually happening was we were cleverly dragging him into our web of womanly charms, woahahahaha. That was supposed to be a haunting and scary laugh and looking at it now all I can hear is Sid James!

I believe Sarah was the chosen one who'd been primed to say she'd like to meet him privately, but it would have to be at his room, so they could have some 'alone time'. He was all for it, of course he was.

The staff rule, no matter which department you worked in was 'no staff allowed in guest rooms'. This was a sack-a-ble offence and that was understandable, there would have been all manner of shenanigans going on otherwise. So yes, we would be breaking the rules, taking a risk, but with good reason, well we felt it was anyhow. The evening arrived and it was time to put our plan into action. As part of the band we finished our last number and the disco took over. I went into the Bronte Bar and the girls had finished their duties and were ready and waiting to play out

'Operation Humiliate Dave', possibly the adult equivalent of the naughty step.

Sarah said "right, come on you lot, I'm going up there now, I've arranged with him to go to his room at midnight, don't leave me". We followed her up the stairs, and as she reached his room we all hid around the corner. We were actually and surprisingly quite nervous, which may explain the strained giggles.

Now the plan was, Sarah would go into his room and then we'd wait 10 minutes. I would then knock on his door saying I really needed to see him, gradually building up his ego so that within an hour there would be a group of us in his room. Confused? Well if you have ever seen a farce in the West End then your half way there. So that's exactly what happened, Sarah went in, I left the 10 minutes gap, then knocked on the door. I pressed my ear to the door and as planned I heard Sarah say,

"Oh no, I'm not s'posed to be in here, I'll get the sack, staff shouldn't be in guest rooms……..what shall I do? Should I get in the wardrobe"?

Eager to keep his female guest 'Dave' agreed "yes, you should". There was a moments silence and then 'Dave' came to the door.

"Er hello" he said peering through a small gap between the door and him.

"Hiya" I replied "you know Monday when you said you'd like to get to know me better, well, here I am 'ta-dah', (yes I actually said ta-dah) just thought that could happen tonight, I've finished work and……..".?

He looked back over his shoulder glancing around his room and said "er yeh, come in".

I really wanted to laugh, but couldn't let everyone down so I thought of every sad thing that's happened to me in my lifetime so that I could focus and remain serious.

We sat on the bed and I did crocodile tears saying I felt I could really talk to him, and I have no idea what I rambled on about but it gave him just cause to put his arm around me, oh behave! Five minutes after this there was a knock at the door.

"Ohhhh whos that" I whispered, looking overly concerned.

"I don't know, I'd better answer it though" he said as the knocking repeated.

"No don't, I shouldn't be here, I work here. I shouldn't be in a guest room" I protested.

"Er, er, well I dunno what to do then". He said standing and half pacing about the room, he looked very worried.

"Shall I just hide under the bed until they've gone"? I suggested.

"Yeh, do that" he said...................Oh please! What an ego.

So I slithered under the bed. He opened the door to Julie. I could hear a bit of flirty chatter and then the door closed and she was in the room and they were both chatting. The boy was very self-assured 'that' I had no doubt about. They both sat on the bed chatting, and I was desperately trying not to laugh. After a few minutes of chat Julie said to him,

"What's up"?

"Nowt" said our little Casanova.

"Well you were all over me this afternoon, do I get a kiss"? She asked.

"Er, yeh" he dithered. It went quiet for a short time (fill in the gap yourself) and directly after this a knock came at the door.

"Oh 'ell, who's this now" he said.

"What do ya mean, who's this now" asked Julie.

"Nothin', nothin', look, can you stand behind the door" he said.

"What"! Said Julie "why do you want me to stand behind the door"?

"Well, you shouldn't really be in here should you" he said, now totally wised up on the hotel rules! Ha.

"Well I will but flaming Nora 'Dave', not nice this ya know" (she was building up her part).

He went over to the door as Julie tucked herself behind it, and opened it up to Michelle standing there.

"Hiya Dave, thought I'd come up and have that drink with ya that ya keep promising".

Whilst he protested scratching his head and saying "eh what's going on here"? Can you believe he still let her in! She was just standing in the doorway and he was nervously holding the door when a crowd of his friends and workmates bombarded the room taking photos and being generally noisy. We'd also planned this with them you see, telling them when to 'attack'. He was red faced and embarrassed and sat on the bed with his head in his hands while his delighted pals jumped around the room and on the bed chanting "Easy, Easy".

By this time I was out from underneath the bed and Sarah and Julie had come out from their hiding places too. He wasn't a bad lad, and took it all in good faith, and hopefully he learned a lesson that day. Either that or it gave him a good story to amuse people for years later.............and if that was the case I'm thinking it was probably exaggerated to seven or eight girls in his room!

The week afterwards we were doing a show and all the workmen were washed, soaked in aftershave, groomed and bellys up at the bar for the evening's duration. We were doing a variety show and it began with three of the girls dancing in stunning feather costumes to the theme music from 'Rocky'. Curtains went back and the lights flooded the stage as the girls walked out one by one to huge cheers from the audience and the workforce alike. I was standing in the wings ready to go out and sing, and the usual cheers I'd heard were par for the course each week. The girls did look beautiful in those pink feather outfits, so it was a noise

I'd become used to. A few moments later and the cheers went up incredibly, 'Ummm unusual, I wonder what's happened' so I did a sneaky peek through the tabs (side stage curtains) and could see all the men at the bar cheering and waving.......and then I spotted Michelle. Her skimpy sparkly bikini top was hanging around her waist, and I think she was going for that whole Les Follies look, Oh la lah! All credit to her, she carried on with the routine, Leeds lass see. As Michelle said herself when she eventually came off the stage,

"I wanted the floor to open up and swallow me, oh the shame. Never mind eh. Oh well if nowt else it made up for us leading 'Dave' on last week".

The following day a little elderly lady walked up to Michelle as she stood selling coach tickets at the information desk.

"Hello dear, could I get a ticket for tomorrow's coach trip, Castle Howard" said the lady.

"Of course you can love" said Michelle "that'll be five pounds please".

As the lady searched in her purse for the correct money she looked up and smiled at Michelle, "We're you the girl who lost her top in the show last night"?

"Yes, that was me" replied Michelle.

"Ohh, nice boobs" said the old dear.

"Owww thank you" said a shocked Michelle.

Possibly the most unusual compliment in that situation she'd ever had. They didn't call it the information desk for nothing!

Quite a few 'unusual' things took place in that hotel.

Like being thrown over the shoulders of a wrestler and being told to "pull my shorts down" where upon doing so it would reveal two eyes, each being tattooed on opposing bottom cheeks! I was acting as a 'Second' during a wrestling 'show'. Part of the choreography was being thrown over the shoulders of wrestler

'Tarantula' (nice man) and having to pull his shorts down.......the guests loved it.........just a regular Sunday afternoon.

Or, morning calls of blowing whistles and ringing bells while walking the corridors of the hotel on Christmas Day morning, often to be met by guests at their room door with a wee dram for the noise offenders..........there were a lot of corridors, 'hic', and sh'lalot of doors 'hic'.

Once in a management meeting as we all sat around the table headed by our G.M. Michael Prendergast (aka Mr. P.) discussing the weeks future events, there was such a noise going on outside on the verandah. The flat roof was being inspected and clearly it was a job that between three men couldn't be done quietly. It went on and on, Mr. P. holding the meeting together but clearly had just about had enough of the interruption when all of a sudden Kay (a lady in every sense of the word. A mature lady who was head of housekeeping, lady of few words in that situation and she resembled a glamorous pub land lady at all times) suddenly stood up, walked over the other side of the room, climbed out of the window! Disappeared out of view........after which we just heard this one sided argument of a female shouting..........................
it all went very quiet. We just heard the tip-tap of her stiletto shoes heading back towards the building. She climbed back in through the window (no one helped, we were all too much in shock), sat down, sniffed, hutched at her boob and said "right then, is it tea break yet".
I miss that lady.

...And now for a sub-title......exciting eh. Yes, sub-title, not to be confused with 'Subway' the sandwich outlet. Handy things though are they not, 'Subway' I mean, especially when you're on the move. I was in-between shows not so long back and with little time to spare for sit down and eat time, it made sense to pop along to the nearest 'Subway' for a sarnie and drink with a fellow singist.

"Ow I flamin' love Subway" she announced "As long as it's not white bread ya laughing"...............

I'll put you straight here and now, there was no laughing when we were presented with our salad filled wholemeal granary! No, no, definitely not. In fact I can't say I've ever laughed at brown bread, or sniggered at a sandwich of any distinction for that matter.

So here we go, sub-title, are you ready?

****

Spooky

Working in the entertainment world there is a lot of behind the scenes stuff that Mr. & Mrs. Audience don't see. The rehearsals, and the rehearsals, oh and the rehearsals! These can happen at any time, mornings, afternoons, in the dead of night, lunch breaks, early hours. Entertainers become obsessed, especially before a new show or routine and if they see an empty room within seconds they can be belting out a song or throwing themselves about with the latest dance routine. One afternoon during a York Races week, which meant the hotel was practically empty each day as 90% of the guests boarded coaches to ferry them to and from York for the racing, my pal Fiona (Fifi to her friends...aka 'Scottish Fiona') had heard the guys from the band, keyboard player Martyn and Drummer Andy were going to be in the building early that afternoon for a band call with a cabaret act.

Andy...(aka my 'bro')....not really but I'd always got along with Andy and the guests seemed to like the fact we were 'siblings'! I introduced him on stage once as "this is Andy my brother, well, my pretend brother". The 'selective hearing group' we're in that evening and decided they only heard the first five words, the 'pretend' bit never happened, and that was that really.

I also randomly announced once (you see 'once' is all it takes) that the sequence dance leaders Charles and Audrey were my 'Sequin Mum and Dad', again, people decided to ignore the sequin bit and presumed they were my parents, it really was a family affair at the Grand!

Where was I, oh yes, so Fifi had previously asked the boys if she could borrow them to play one song so that she could record it and then have it on tape in order to learn for a new show that was in the pipeline. They agreed, and so did I, as she needed me to sing it for her. This happened in the main ballroom. The ballroom is quite rare for a hotel, as it's like a small theatre, ground level seating and dancefloor with a stage, and then a seating dress circle, the ceiling being three times plus the height of a regular ballroom, great acoustics thanks to its dome shape, really quite beautiful. We stood on the stage and with song recorded Martyn and Andy left the room which left Fi and myself, we just sat on the edge of the stage chatting when all of a sudden we both, without any prompt to each other, looked up to the dress circle. There was a small woman in what looked like a pale pink crinoline dress, she suddenly did an about turn, and although there are three doors that lead onto the circle at its own level, she went through the wall (I do hope you're not reading this in a darkened room). Neither of us said anything, we just stood up and rushed to the side doors of the ballroom and rushed up the narrow stone steps (not used by the public) leading up to the first floor/dress circle. On getting there she had completely disappeared. We looked over the balcony that gave a clear view of the foyer and the grand staircase but she was nowhere to be seen. Even if she'd have run, we would have still seen her on the balcony, and with no guests in the building to speak of there was no background noise or music on, so we would've heard if she'd have gone into any of the rooms. It was a while before either of us said anything. Then fi said in her lovely Scottish accent,

"Did ya just see what I think 'I' just saw"?

The answer to that was, "yes, I did".

Neither of us felt frightened, I mean "Owwwwoooo (that was me doing a ghost noise) scary stuff, a lady in a pretty frock".

We'd have been far more frightened of 'maniac on the first floor wielding an axe'.

We did tell some other staff who, it has to be said, felt the need to take the mickey out of us, and a few who 'said' they didn't believe us, but wouldn't go to the costume storage room a floor below ground level on their own again! It wasn't really until day turned into night, and night turned into, well, later that night that it gave us time to think and be a little bit scared. But we know what we saw.

I said to Fi, "I wonder if she used to work here when the hotel opened and she just came for a visit?"

Fi said "well we don't mind that, but a little bit of warning would have been nice, how the heck am I going to sleep in this place tonight?"

I think our disappearing lady just popped in knowing it would help Fi. You see that December we performed 'Cinderella'. Oh yes we d...............(No, I refuse to start that) at the hotel as one of the shows and Fi made Sarah (who played Cinderella) her

wedding/ball gown and it looked rather similar to our visitors pale pink dress.

Quite a few of the staff and guests had said how they had witnessed some strange and un-explainable sightings at The Grand. The night doorman once accosted a young man as he just walked through the main doors and up the staircase in the early hours, but as the doorman reached the bottom of the stairs calling "excuse me are you a guest sir", the young man just completely disappeared into thin air. As the doorman said, by the time I'd reached the bottom of the stairs even if he'd have run up the stairs he still wouldn't have been at the top (do you need to put extra lights on? still Okay? Yes? Then I'll carry on).

The hotel had so many nooks and crannies that you could work there months, possibly years and never have been in every single part of the hotel. It's huge. There are, however some floors below the ground level, as we know it, that haven't been used in years. One particular floor has the original kitchens and I'm not quite sure why, but when I worked there and ventured to this baron space there were still things out on the work tops and tables, cups, plates etc, as if the people working there at the time had suddenly heard a fire-alarm or something and run out of the building never to return, very weird.

This floor was used for a 'ghost walk' that the entertainment staff would do once a week during the winter months. When I was entertainment manager I didn't do duties as such, but there was a bug going around and it had taken quite a few of my team, making them very poorly and leaving me with less than half my staff. My assistant Steve (aka 'the wizard of the neck and shoulder massage') had said during this particular morning how maybe we should cancel the ghost walk as there were no staff available to do it. I said "No it's ok, I'll do it". Steve said "Oh great, I was trying to work out 'how could I do 'Hoy' and the ghost walk' at the same time".

As it turned out, no guests turned up for Hoy, so Steve came walking into the foyer looking a little redundant while I waited for guests interested in joining me. As he walked towards me saying "I may as well come 'n' do the ghost walk with ya", four guests also arrived in front of us asking for the ghost walk.

"Yes, that's us" I said. We stood and chatted waiting an extra five minutes to see if anyone else was going to turn up.

"I think we can go then" I said to the two couples consisting of two gents and two ladies. Steve and I guided them down the back staircase, usually reserved only for staff members or maintenance, we went further and further down.

After a while the service lights stopped and it was torches on. "Oh I don't know if I like this" said one of the ladies.

Her husband replied "I know, you'd have thought they'd have painted these stairs wouldn't ya"

But I don't think that was what she meant.

As you get further down into the building due to the thick walls and heavy doors the other sounds at the main entrance ground level gradually evaporate and all you can hear apart from the sound of your own breathing and footsteps is the odd squeak and creek of the hotel!

When we did these 'walks' depending on who was playing tour guide, some of the 'reds' would tell fabricated ghost stories, and others like myself would talk about a little of the history of the building. Steve and I were quite good at this as we became the equivalent of a historian Morecambe and Wise (comedy double act) and would make it entertaining for the guests. The tour, chat included I'd say, would usually take anything from 40 minutes to an hour. After around 20 minutes of the six of us shuffling about in the dark with just torch light, Steve said "Ow I did say I'd help Michelle get some of the costumes up from wardrobe for the show tonight if Hoy didn't go ahead, I hope she's not waiting, is it alright if I go".

"Yeh, that's alright, off you go". I said.

He walked back to where we'd come from and we could hear his footsteps as they became fainter making his way back up the stairs.

We were having a steady walk down a corridor and as previously instructed I reminded the small group.

"Please don't wander through any of the open doors, some of the flooring isn't safe, if we all keep close together there won't be any accidents", bearing in mind, the only light down there was any natural light that had managed to peep through windows, other than that is was me and my hand held torch.

All of a sudden one of the women screamed.

"Arrrrrrrrrrrrrhhhhhhhhhhhh". The others laughed, be it nervous hysteria type laughter.

"Are you alright" I asked, thinking she'd seen a mouse (there was the odd one that had taken up residency).

"Down there, down there" she said pointing in front of us "down there, there's a man". I shone my torch to show the length of the corridor.

"Don't be daft" said her husband "You've been watching too many horror films, there's nothing down there, it's probably a mirror n you've caught a reflection" he continued.

"It's not a mirror, it was a man" she said, visibly shaken.

I shone the torch around but couldn't see anything.

I called out "Steve………Steve, are you playing silly beggers"?

There was no reply.

"Come on" I said sensing the lady was spooked "I know it's called a ghost walk, that's just to get you interested, but we're usually treated to cobwebs and flatulence down here, that's about as scary as it gets".

Shining the torch to guide us we all carried on walking forwards, I continued telling them about different historical aspects of the hotel and another ten minutes had passed by when all of a sudden there was a 'BANG' and ahead of us right at the end of the corridor we all stood transfixed as a figure (presuming a man) came out of one door and straight over the corridor into another room.

"ARRRRRRRRRRHHHHHHHHHHHHHHHHH", screamed the ladies........and you know that thing on a ship about 'woman and children first', well it didn't apply in this case. No sooner had we seen the tall dark figure ahead of us, the men had pushed by their ladies and torch or no torch they rushed up the stairs leaving their wives with me! Both of the ladies grabbed hold of my arms and with torch as guide we too quickly made our way back rushing up the stairs.

We arrived in the foyer to see their husbands at the bar ordering drinks. Relieved at being back in the land of the three dimensional people the ladies laughed off the incident and sat on the large leather sofas telling some other guests about their spooky ordeal. As this was happening I spotted Steve coming out of the ballroom.

"Oi, Steve, come here" I called. "What have you been up to"? I said smiling "you frightened me to death. My guests almost had kittens down there"

"Eh, I don't know what you mean"? He said.

I laughed, "No of course you don't. I wish you'd have let me in on your plan, I could've hammed it up a bit more, although doubt they would've hung around to see what was going to happen next". Steve stood there with a confused look on his face.

"I have no idea what you're going on about" he said.

It was then I realized how on earth did he get changed so fast and get back up the stairs before me. The route we used to take for the ghost walk was the only way you could get up and down to that floor, so he would have had to pass us....twice.

"Oh no" I said "I think, er, I think".

"What? What do you think"? He asked.

So I explained what had just happened.

"No...not me. I've been up here all the time with Michelle, sorting out these costumes for tonight". Michelle then came out of the ballroom and asked if everything was alright.

"Has at any point in the past 15 minutes Steve left your sight"? I asked kind of wanting the answer to be yes.

She said 'No, we've been putting the costumes into the dressing rooms for the show later".

(........you still alright?............'what was that noise'?.......no it's okay, it was just something outside).

We never did get to the bottom of what we saw, and we 'did' see something, all five of us.

The following day a few of the chaps, staff that is, ventured down to the floor to do a little investigating, but it was a little like closing the stable door once the horse had bolted really.

I never did do another ghost walk...........Actually, I don't think there was ever another ghost walk in the hotel, not in my time there at any rate. The attitude of the 'reds' seem to go like this, "No, don't believe in ghosts me, right load of rubbish, but, er, it might be a bit dangerous going down those stone stairs so we'd better stay up here. Nothing to see down there anyhow, and I have to be careful with my leg 'n' everything, so er, shall we do chair bingo instead"!!!

****

186

If Steve had of been hiding in the shadows (which to this day he assures me he didn't..........and I believe him) then it would be understandable, why? Well, we did a potted tribute show of 'Les Miserables'. In it I doubled up as Fantine and Madam Thenardier. During a scene in which Madam 'T' welcomed a traveler into her establishment for refreshment, well that traveler was Steve and the refreshment was supposed to be gruel. That particular set on stage was so close to the audience we agreed that instead of pretending, he should actually be served some food, of sorts. So I suggested the cereal 'Wheatabix' soaked in water. We did a few weeks of this, and then the naughty mischief fairies suggested in my ear that I add sugar to it, quite a lot of sugar. I'll cut a long story short, the sugar became more and more and more, then salt and pepper was introduced, gravy granules, ...various ingredients were added of a herbidacious (pronounced her-be-day-shsssshh – as in keep it quiet) nature, until one night it was curry powder. The poor lad, I stood there 'singing and grumbling' as Mrs. 'T', and as I looked across the stage at Steve eating the concoction, I swear I saw steam coming out of his ears.

Sorry Steve, I bet he never forgot that show. ☺ So you see had he been our mysterious phantom then it would only have been some sweet revenge, and they do say it's a dish best served cold..........or in his case hot hot hot.........again..........sorry Steve.

Meanwhile during less spiritually and mouthwateringly challenged times, the Grand played host to many a top cabaret artiste, and they didn't come any better than singer/comedian/impressionist Paul Squire. So good was his act that after the song and dance routine that myself and Michelle would perform each Sunday as the opener to his show we would rush to change and get to the back of the ballroom so that we could stand and watch this first class act over and over again. It just never got old. Always as entertaining and funny and each week he would add a new gag in his routine stating afterwards "there you go, one for the staff". One of the finest cabaret acts I've ever been fortunate enough to work alongside, a true expert at his craft.

The night before this particular Sunday we'd performed an old time music hall……..or for those of you in the know, a 'Ye Olde Music Hall'. It was full of what you would expect of a music hall. Songs that they 'just don't write 'em like that anymore', comedy, sketches, dance routines plus a dance that I was also part of, the Can-Can, which I just couldn't-couldn't do now. One of the sketches ended with the shooting of a starting pistol, how ironic, and so we had one that we used with blanks, as opposed to real bullets, as if we would? But strangely I still felt the need to explain that.

It was kept in a high security box with lock and key and that in turn was kept in a room where you needed a code at the door. Oh sorry, no it wasn't, it was left wherever, er, it was left. (I can hear health and safety sorts having palpitations as I write) Back then health and safety consisted of "Ave ya pu'rit down?" "Yeh"……"alright then". Things were far more………relaxed.

On this occasion I speak of, it had been left on a shelf in the wings, very naughty. Nothing to do with me I might add. If I'd have been in charge at that point it would've been under lock and key for sure.

Michelle and I were in the dressing room getting dolled up to the nines, me in my full length red sequin halter neck dress and Michelle in a saucy little gold sequin number.

"Is Paul here"? Asked Michelle,

"Yeh, he's been here since around 5, there's some chap with him, p'raps his manager?" I told her.

The band struck up and played the overture 'Axel F', so with stage curtains drawn I walked over to the opposite side of the stage and stood in the wings waiting to go on. Michelle stood in the wings from where I'd just come from and was smiling and pointing behind me. I turned around to find Mr. Squire pulling faces behind me,

"Hello" I said in his ear.

"Hiya love, ya alright" he answered back.

"Yeh, I'm good ta" I replied.

"What's happening now then, you doing a song"? he asked.

"Yes, a new one this week" I said. "I'm singing 'The Man with the Golden Gun' and Michelle's doing a dance routine".

"Oh right" he replied, and with that he mouthed 'hello' over the stage to Michelle and waved.

The overture was coming to an end and the curtains began to slowly open. Michelle and I gave each other the thumbs up as Paul and his guest asked "what's this used for", picking up the starting pistol.

Turning around, I quickly answered......"Music hall gag"

As the curtains fully opened, the overture stopped and Paul shot the pistol pointing it to the floor, not realizing (as neither did I) that it still had a blank left in it.

'B-A-N-G', it boomed out 'SO LOUD' backstage, on the stage and the sound r-a-n-g around the ballroom.............As it BANGED the pressure of the gun firing had an adverse effect on my frock, and the halter neck just broke.......'SNAP'.....and woohoo! The things my Mother had always told me to keep covered up were now out and on show.

Quite possibly due to the theme of the show opening song the audience may have presumed this gun shot was part of the show, let's hope eh.

189

Michelle stood open mouthed as the 'da-da-da-da-da' of the music that began the song, rang out, played by the band.

Due to holding a radio microphone I struggled to get hold of both parts of the halter neck and do a make-shift strap holding it behind my neck. The clasp that had held it together was no longer there. I gingerly stepped onto the stage into the bright lights holding my dress up, and Michelle who should have at this point been at the far front of the stage had seen my predicament and had 'step-ball-changed' her way over to me. She grabbed hold of the straps and followed me onto the stage, whilst holding my dignity intact, and yes, she did still do a dance routine of sorts whilst attached 'to' me, waving her left arm/hand about in double time. My faithful 'Spectrum Dancer'.

I have no idea what the audience thought was going on, I sang but starred at the back wall of the room. I couldn't even glance at Michelle as I knew that would send me into hysterics, and she didn't look at me, especially when I started with the opening lyrics to the song............

"He has a powerful weapon"......................no Mrs...........please don't.

We got through the whole song. How? I will never know.

Professional types us ya know.

The only part that did look very suspect and totally out of place was at the end of the song where I introduced Paul, with Michelle still standing right at the side of me with her hand at the back of my neck. We'd never have passed for Ray Allen and Lord Charles....."ya silly ar*e".

We then scuttled off the stage with shuffling baby steps like Siamese twins as Paul walked by taking the radio mic from me and laughing............to 'his' opening lyrics......."Once in a lifetime, a man has a moment"......

On getting to the safety of the dressing room we both sat on the floor laughing to the point of tears.

"Michelle, the man with the golden gun hee hee hee" I said.

"I know" she laughed. "We're never going to forget this Shelley" stated Michelle.

No............and we never have.

Do you have any unusual memorable moments from staying in a hotel and/or watching a show?

Favourite overheard quote of the time.

".....well I was going to come with my husband but I'm here with a friend. Daft begger forgot to put his holidays in at work. Useless he is. He couldn't organize a pair of socks."

Chapter Fourteen... Strange Magic

In the 80's I came across a feature in the Nottingham Evening Post which caught my eye. It was a picture story of a very slim, attractive young woman advertising for someone to do a double act with her in the form of fire-eating and illusion. In the photograph she is holding her head back with fire torch poised in front of her, dressed in a rather snazzy outfit. 'Oh that looks interesting' I thought, and a few days later with the story still floating around my head I decided to see what it was all about so gave the newspaper a ring and they put me in contact with the young lady in the photograph, Liz. A few days after this we met and over a coffee or three she told me about her hopes for the act.

"How many people have you had contact you" I asked.

"Oh you and a chap that didn't really know why he'd contacted me" she said.

With that sort of competition I couldn't help but think 'This is in the bag' ha ha. We sat and chatted all afternoon and I really liked her, her style and her plans, so we decided there and then together we'd give the idea a go.

I'd been singing as a solo act for a few years and everyone to their own, but I'd discovered I seemed happier when I was part of a band, cast etc. I knew that I'd always have my own act, but if there was a chance to do something different that involved others now and again then I was up for it.

Over the next few weeks we got together and rehearsed our fire/illusion/dance/singing act. Liz had had a sub-trunk made, and for those of you that think "eh? What's one of those when it's at home", let me tell you, you do know what they are! They are the large boxes that the magicians use. One lady goes in the box and another gets up on top of the box, surrounds herself with a curtain like screen, drops the curtain and the lady that 'was' in the box is now on top of the box, and the one that was on top of the box is now in the box..........simple.

So we rehearsed and rehearsed........We tried many combinations but it appeared for whatever reason it was best she went in the box first and I was the one that would get up onto the box with the curtain like thingy. Oh if only I could do that now, not with my back!

We rehearsed the whole 50 minute show which was all set to music, and so I would sing, Liz would fire-eat and she'd taught me how to 'body burn'! No, it's not getting too close to the fire after you've been outside in the cold. You take a lit fire wand and roll it up and down your arms or legs, whatever takes ya fancy. DON'T TRY THIS AT HOME.

So a few times a week or as much as our individual lives would allow we would get together and rehearse in a church hall close by to where Liz lived. We hit it off from the word go, so the rehearsal days were never a drag, always enjoyable. It eventually came to the date of our first gig. It was good! To say we had only just met a couple of months before, it flowed quite nicely and all went to plan..........I sang, Liz fire-ate, we body burned and went in and out of the sub-trunk like we'd done it all our lives. Hey, we did it. So, happy girls and soon after this we did the done thing and got appropriate publicity photos done, all very seductively mysterious with 'up' lighting. Oh and we decided on a name 'Lizelle'.........get us!

We did a few gigs and then were advised to 'do a showcase'. This is where you do approximately 10-15 minutes of your act sharing the stage with other acts doing the same on that night. So we got ourselves booked onto a showcase and knowing how the sub-trunk took up a lot of stage we decided it could have the night off and we'd just do two songs and Liz performing some fire-eating. We looked so glitz and glam, how could the agents in the audience fail but want to see more of our act and book us. So there we were sharing the stage with two other singers and several bands. Two drum kits filled the back area of the stage and guitars stretched the length and depth of the stage so there was precious little room for anything else........Please leave egos at the door, I thaaaank yoooou.

The singers were a male/female act and then......us.

Although we weren't doing the sub trunk this particular night, where he would often 'give us a lift with it', my Dad and his friend had come along just to watch the showcase. The show began and a very jolly round compare bounced onto the stage in a rather loud jacket to introduce the first act......

"Evening ladies and gentlemen" he said "well here we are, showcase time and have we got some great acts for you..........I don't know.........Have we got any great acts for them"? (he said, looking into the wings of the stage).

That was the first time I'd ever heard that line........and not the last........I've even been known to use it myself. Well, if you can't beat 'em..............

The first band did their bit, and very good they were too. Then another band, in fact 4 bands went on before us, followed by the duo, and then it was our turn. As we sat in the dressing room Liz filled the goblet she used for the act with paraffin for lighting the fire wands.

"That's quite full" I remember saying.

"Oh it'll be alright, I need the wands soaked" she said.

'Ummm, Ok.....she knows what she's doing', I thought. And she did, Liz was great at the old fire eating. We got onto the stage as our compare was giving us the big build up, Liz placed the goblet on the floor just behind us, and the music track kicked in.......so I began to sing, Liz doing a little dancy routine to this. I was very conscious that we needed to be careful not to knock the goblet over, so kept inching forwards as much as I could without falling off the front of the stage. All going well, then the second section of music began for the next song. During this there was a long instrumental bit where Liz would do her fire eating expertise, and I would do one of two things, pose at the side of the stage or just go in the wings. Well I sang as much as I needed to and I could feel behind me the heat as Liz set up the fire wands. My part ended, so I decided the safest thing to do was to move into the wings not having much room on the stage. The lights went down and it looked amazing. Liz having this gazelle like stature and the fire wheel spinning around, in her hands, then her mouth, it really was a fantastic spectacle. The flames looked incredible as did she......she spun, she danced, she spun some more and 'plink'.......she 'just' caught the side of the goblet with the heal of her shoe, it rocked, it spun a little, it rocked back again and then 'tilt', 'plonk', 'whoooooosh'.

The goblet lay on the stage, paraffin rather majestically gliding along towards all the instruments almost as if it 'knew' which direction it 'shouldn't' be traveling in.

'Ohhhh heck, I just hope that'............and at that exact moment of my thoughts a tiny spark from the fire wheel gently floated down onto the travelling stream of paraffin and 'whooooooosh' again, except this time in the form of flames. The stage being practically in darkness this looked really impressive!.....for all of 3 seconds, and then the reality hit. I rushed onto the stage, when I say 'rushed' it all went into slow motion, and my legs just didn't seem to go fast enough, it was like running through gravy. However over towards the instruments I flew and one by one grabbed as many of the guitars standing on their little stands for 'safety', as I could, I managed to carry five! (Guitars by the way can be quite heavy). A right hullabaloo then followed as the recognition of what was actually happening on the stage dawned on the audience and you could see by the reactions of the faces looking up at us exactly who owned the guitars!!!

As I was heading towards the wings, instruments in hand I spotted my Dad's face as he sat in the centre of the room and I mouthed 'D-A-D...h-e-l-p'.......He stood up and with pal John and they literally ran across the tables in front of the stage mouthing back.... "b-l-e-e-p-i-n-g 'e-l-l". He along with several other chaps pulled down the tab curtains and doused out the fire. During all this the music carried on and Liz, bless her heart carried on with the act! Agents in the audience you see, so one should never miss an opportunity.

Band members were scurrying onto the stage and the likes of my Dad and others were making sure everything was safe. Liz came off the stage complete with soot-smudged face, and the jolly compare tip toed onto the stage announcing,

"Well girls you nearly brought the house down with that act" ....and the audience chortled, probably with relief.

Liz came into the band room where I'd decided seconds before to take refuge with guitars, and her face was of shock and surprise.

"Oh heck, owah, what happened" she said.

"The paraffin happened" I replied, "You caught it with your heel and wallop, it was gone".

Due to the fact no one was harmed and no instruments were damaged I can look back on this now as a total one off incident that I know I shall never experience again, no really, I can, because you couldn't make up this kinda stuff.

But I did do something that night I'd never done before or since actually. I refused to go out on the stage at the end of the show and take a bow. Very un-professional I know, but I just couldn't face the audience. That venue could have been a right off, or even worse, and we could have been on the national news! So no, I just couldn't face it (sorry Liz). I don't remember if we got any work from that showcase. Not sure if anyone was brave enough to take us on, think of the insurance.

That aside we did have some nice gigs, and at most I took a bow at the end!!!

There was one however, which could've quite easily popped up on a comedy programme.......I'm thinking the Peter Kay classic 'Phoenix Nights'.

We'd been booked for a gig 'up't north'. When you're previously told "Oh the audiences up there can be difficult sometimes", it doesn't really fill you with confidence, but we were young and hungry for success and so we took on the booking. Arriving at the club we were met by the 'concert secretary' who had all the charm of a lamp post, but again, you put it down to experience and get on with the job the best way you can.

This was a full show, so before the audience came in we set up our things on the stage, the sub-trunk, fire wands, costumes etc, and that was that, stage set. We just needed to get ready in our gold and red sparkly outfits and we were good to go.

We could hear the audience filling the room from the dressing room and the chairman kept knocking on the door, with his version I presume of a pep talk.

"Arrr, they're nearly all in, not be long now, the fish mans just going round", he said.

"Eh"???

Soon after, he'd be tapping at the door again.

"Do ya sell anything? We don't like it when people try to sell things, we don't need anything".

Well no, we didn't sell anything, so we told him this.

"Arrrhhh good" he replied "Cos wer' sick of folk tryin' ta sell records (records!!?...around this time cassettes were 'the thing') n' such like, we don't need it". He spoke for his people.

Having no real welcome at this venue we felt at least we were slightly in favour by not peddling goods.......maybe?

Ten minutes later he was at the door again, "Three minutes and we'll be ready for ya, Bob's just selling the meat raffle tickets, not be long now, then ya can get it over with".

Get it over with! Wow, with this sort of build up how could we fail.

The time finally arrived,

"Right then girls, we're ready for ya" he said and off we trotted to the wings. This was a big club with a huge stage and we'd been told when full it was a 250 audience. It was a Friday night and our 'chairman' had told us it was practically sold out due to our act. Apparently our posters had created much interest. Oh the pressure.

With raffle tickets sold, we heard the rumble of voices gradually go quiet as our introduction started.

"Good Evening Ladies and Gents, right then, got a couple of young lasses here from Nottingham (a few boos were heard!)...now then, now don't be like that, and they're here to show us what they can do"............It was practically Palladium standard.

Music started, curtains opened, we walked out to a sea of faces and bright lights, I began to sing and Liz danced..........................

.................................The audience........not exactly what you would call encouraging, but they sat and watched, a lot of folded arms, but they still sat............and watched.

During my second song the young man at the lighting desk was having a field day, obviously there hadn't been such an act like ours that had donned the stage in quite some time and I'm presuming he'd been resigned to the odd light change and follow

spot on a regular basis, so we were getting the works. On the way home Liz referred to it as 'a demonstration of what the lights were capable of'.

Songs done, and a bit of chat introducing the fire-eating.........Torches lit, lights down, and although I say so myself, it looked pretty darn impressive.

The audience..........sat and watched.

As this was a big venue Liz did the fire breathing at the end of this section. I'll explain, you basically fill your mouth with paraffin, then spit-spray it out whilst holding a lit torch ahead of you to create a huge gust of flame........'tis rather impressive.

The audience..........sat..............and watched.

The time came for our sub-trunk illusion. Now we'd begun to get so fast with this, we'd now up-graded to not only getting in and out and out and in, we were also changing outfits! Yes, you did read that correctly, whilst 'in' the box, we would change into different outfits. While we'd go in covered in red and gold glitz, we would emerge in black and white sparkles, of opposite colours to style of outfit if that makes sense. I guess like a negative to photo. This was always responded with an "Oowww" from the audiences. Yes our finale definitely had the 'Wow' factor, or maybe on this occasion, the 'why' factor.

First things first, we got a gent up out of the audience to prove that our handcuffs were the real thing.....no velcro to see here. With gent safely back in his seat the music began, we danced around the back and then opposite sides of the sub-trunk and met at the front of it where we gracefully opened up the trunks lid, and it sat upright presenting its plush interior. I picked up the handcuffs and placed them around Liz's wrists and 'clicked' them to lock. We did a little dance, and then Liz stepped into the trunk while I.......danced some more. While she was seductively

200

moving with her hands held above her head I reached over the edge of the trunk and lifted up the sack that she was now standing in. I raised it and raised it until she bobbed down a little and I was able to tie the red velvet ribbon at the top, and with that gently pushed her down into the trunk. That done I danced around the other side of the trunk, got hold of the lid and closed the trunk, reached for the lock on a side stand, hooked it onto the trunks lid and 'clunk', it was locked. I then.......danced some more at the same time showing the audience the key to the lock which had been sitting with the lock on the side stand. (...are you O.K. following this???).......As I did this, something felt amiss, but I didn't worry too much........probably just the audience not giving much feedback I thought (but at least they were still watching). I popped the key back onto the side table and the music kicked in with dramatic build up........owwwww.

The curtain screen sat on a hoop around the trunk which sat on the floor and I grabbed hold of it and then popped myself up onto the top of the trunk.............Now, as a rule, it went something like this....Liz would hear me getting on top of the trunk, I would count to 3, shimmy the curtain up and over the top of my head, bring it down and shout ""ONE.....................hold the curtain up above my head ....''TWO''............................and 'she' would shout "THREE" bringing the curtain down, and the swap transformation would have been done. Liz would then drop the curtain hoop, jump down from the trunk, meanwhile I would be 'in' the trunk, she would unlock the trunk, I would stand up, she would untie the sack, I would appear with handcuffs on, she would unlock handcuffs I would climb out of trunk in an ever so stylish manner, we would pose, take a bow, audience would go wild. It was fabulous darrrrling.

On this particular night……..It didn't quite happen like that! But my reader friends, it did happen, er, like this.

I got up onto the trunk with hoop in hand, and the counting began, I shimmied the curtain up and over the top of my head, I brought it down and shouted "ONE"…………I held the curtain up above my head…….."TWO"……………I shimmied it down again…………."THREE"……..I shimmied it up again ………….. "FOUR"?……….I shimmied it down again………………er, "five"???……………I then proceeded with no sign of Liz, to shimmy to the music…….""Shimmy, shimmy, shimmy"""…………."""shimmy, shimmy"""………"""shimmy"""…………………….."'sh-im----my'". Nothing was happening………..I stamped my foot onto the lid in an attempt to rush Liz along. The shimmying continued. Still nothing happening, except for, hang on a minute, what was that muffled sound I could hear coming from the trunk?

It sounded like….."I caaamb…….geeeeed……….ouuuuuuddd"?….I shimmied some more and the curtain flapped about like we were sailing on the ocean wave, which brings the phrase to mind, 'worse things happen at sea'.

I decided (whilst shimmy'ing my backside off) to get down from the top of the trunk………still 'presenting'….still shimmying….and placed the curtain at an angle over the trunk. Trying to think what to do next, I decided, dance…..maybe I could hear what the muffles were if I just danced next to the trunk.

"Liz" I called while I covered my face with a seductive impromptu dance move!

"LIZ" I called out for a second time…….again came back the mumble. "I caaamb…..geeeeed…..ouuuuud".

I danced around the other side, arms up, arms to the side……la di dah………arms down, la di dah, arms generally flapping about………….."I caaanb geed oouutttdd" I heard again, except this time I'd figured out what she was trying to say.

Oh no........she can't get out!!! How come this story was never featured in a 'Lassie' film?!

What do I do now?

There wasn't much I could do to save the situation, the music was on the verge of ending, Liz was still in the trunk, I'd shimmied and danced about using every dance movement possible in the history of dancing........I somehow had to get the trunk to the back of the stage! So I tried to drag it there. Don't judge me please you luckily didn't have my problem. Thankfully Liz was about 6 stone wet through, but the trunk was not............I began to pull the trunk, heavvveeeeee, and heavvveeeeee, the trunk squeaking its way to the back of the stage with me heave hoe'ing, sweat pouring off me.

The audience sat..........and watched.

THERE NOW FOLLOWS A SPOILER WARNING..........LOOK AWAY FROM THE BOOK IF YOU DON'T WANT TO KNOW THE FOLLOWING....................

It was no good, I had to get Liz out of the trunk, so I slid the trap door at the back of the trunk open (sorry folks, it ain't real magic) and out she tumbled, half in, half out the sack. All the time whilst doing this I was bending down and popping up again in a dancy'fied (a technical term in the world of entertainment) manner. This was now with no music I might add, but I had to just let the audience know I was still there.

So I lah-di-dah'ed as loud as I could!

Liz wriggled out of the sack, handcuffs still on, both now puffing and panting we then stood up at the back of the trunk.............smiled, and posed!!!

..............................waited...

.......................and the audience sat...........and watched.

We held our pose breathing like we'd just finished a marathon as the chairman walked onto the stage to the sound of his own footsteps with microphone in hand, lassoing the mic lead towards the ground as he walked in front of us and said,
"well ladies and gents, there ya go, 'Lizelle'....we've never had anything like that here, now have we, thank you girls".
The room was hushed apart the clink of glasses in the distance and from a minor few who clapped and the odd cough. The curtains eventually closed, 'squeak, squeak, squeak' to the dumbfounded room. We then scuttled around the stage area hunting for correct keys to open locks!
For some unknown reason we'd set the keys in the wrong order, instead of leaving the keys to the handcuffs inside the trunk, that was the key we'd left on the side stand, and the key 'to' the trunk, blissfully unaware, sat 'inside' the trunk. Not much use when you need them the other way around, but nice we'd discovered our mistake. After this fiasco we tied bright coloured ribbons on the keys, one in blue, one in red. Isn't it amazing how we can always manage to solve a problem.........once it's happened.
Feeling rather deflated we got back into the dressing room, with no chat, got changed, packed all the props away from the stage area and then back into the dressing room to check we hadn't left anything behind.......you know......like a key, dignity or something! There was a tap tap tap at the door.
"Hello" came a now familiar voice, "just me" said the chairman.
"Right then, I owe you young ladies some money", and he perched himself on the dressing table corner and counted out our fee.
We both thanked him, (not expecting to be paid actually) and then he reached into his top pocket took out a diary and said "Now then, let me see, we want to get you back later in the year, October looks favourite, so what available dates do you have"?

..................................We both sat in shock and looked at each other. Had he been in a different room when we did our act?........and when I say act, I mean, focusing on the sub trunk illusion. The illusion here being, 'did he think that's how it was supposed to happen'?
I couldn't help myself, I had to ask,
"Are you sure you want us back? The audience, they didn't 'really' clap at all".
"Ow don't worry about that, they don't", came back his reply.
"But they didn't throw anything at ya either, and they stayed for the duration, so they must've liked ya" he said.
We traveled home that night in a very confused state.

We never did go back and perform at that club.
Liz and I parted company about eight months later, no drastic fallout. More and more venues sadly had decided not to use speciality acts. Most now leaning towards self-contained singers or comedians, acts with tracks! We felt our act had just gone its natural distance. I ventured down south to do a season singing with a band, and the last I heard from Liz she was dancing on a cruise ship.
I did see her very briefly in the early 1990's, I was at Attenborough Nature Reserve with some of my family having an afternoon out, and I noticed this young woman jogging by and at the point where I realized it was Liz, there she was...........gone. I have to say I sort of like the fact that we didn't go back to the northern club, we did have a date fixed but we politely cancelled about 3 months after, deciding, best leave that memory intact. It's been forever frozen in time as the venue that saw the alternative version of the sub trunk illusion. How strange that along with the very first time we did it, the 'alternative'

performance is the one that remains at the forefront of my mind.

And I'm glad I met Liz be it for a short period of my life, we shared some very enjoyable and new adventures together and she was the first person that introduced me to veggie burgers!

So have a think, what's the strangest specialty act you've ever seen?

Favourite overheard quote of the time.

"Oww for an ugly bloke Jackie he was quite good looking when he put his mind to it."

Chapter Fifteen... Lady In Red

Have you ever had a box full of puppies, started to play with them and then 'tried' to get them all back into the box? No? Well how about a true story going back to my school days when I 'rescued' 32 frogs from the schools science lab, all due to be cut into tiny pieces the following day. I might add the nerves on this day were off the scale, totally out of character to go against school rules and afterwards went home and sobbed at the kitchen table as I explained to Mum why I was so late, even though in my heart I felt I'd done the right thing. My head was confusing me as this felt so right yet I felt I'd also done wrong. Basically I hid in the toilets after school, climbed into the classroom over the door through the window, jumped down the other side snagging my school blouse en route, got all the frogs in my bag, my pockets etc, and then climbing out of another window made my way to the local park where I let them all go near the pond.

I stood shaking myself as they all popped out of pockets and sleeves, and I possibly looked like I'd just been covered with itching powder. For a split second they all just stood and looked at me, probably a bit dazed at their fortune I'd like to think. Then they all jumped off in different directions and I remember thinking "oh well, there's no way I'm going to be able to get them back now".........a box of puppies, pockets full of frogs, a group of folk of a 'er, more mature age' (as you will see in a paragraph or two) Same thing!!!

Over the next week at school, I'd have teachers passing me in the corridor saying "hello Shelley" accompanied by a little wink or nod.

'Did they know? Or didn't they know', I'd keep asking myself. Then a new assistant teacher that had been with the school approximately two weeks took our class for dance/drama. As she went around the pupils asking our names, when she arrived at me she said,

"Oh so you're Shelley are you, I've heard a lot about you this week in the staff room, your quite famous" and thankfully she smiled.

Me....*Hums a tune in head and looks out of window*

Life has certainly taken some strange twists and turns, example, I'd been teaching a group of over 65's for a one off concert they'd been asked to do. This was a little spin off group from a local amateur dramatics society I'd just choreographed a show for, and I'd been asked in a professional capacity if I would coach them for said concert. I'd agreed thinking "well, it all sounds rather laid back, gentle, how difficult could it be", and with that I took the extra work on.

The lessons, which consisted of 2 days each week, came with their own set of little dramas. Like Olive getting the wrong days of the week, most weeks. Harry losing his bus pass over and over again, and Doris, forgetting her teeth on one memorable occasion. In a relatively short space of time I got used to them, (the members, not Doris' teeth!) and they got used to me, we compromised.

Anyhow the day of the concert arrived. We'd decided sensibly as the group were amateur singers we would have a lesson directly before the concert during the afternoon. That way everything would be fresh in their minds for the evening performance.

The lesson was 1pm – 4pm and I decided to get there a little earlier just to be on the safe side and be super duper organized for the group arriving. Sure enough they began to trickle in at 12.30 and Maureen who'd had a birthday 2 days previous had kindly brought in a big box of cakes for everyone. As people arrived she proudly announced,

"Oh I've brought cake for everyone, cake, over here, cake", and then in zombie like fashion, they all just dropped their coats, bags and wandered over to the lady with the cakes....I looked at my watch, "nah, don't worry Shelley" I thought, "it's only 5 minutes to, even if we start at ten past, we'll be fine and they will be ready and raring to go". The cake was obviously far more important than I'd given it credit, as it came with a side order of in depth detail about the cake maker (her daughter-in-law) the birthday party (the night previous), the guests at the birthday party and it seemed a detailed description of each and every card she had received for this prestigious 75th birthday..........................

It was now 20 minutes past 1pm.

"Ok everyone, Maureen how lovely you've had such a smashing week, and I'm sure I speak for everyone when I say thank you for the cake, but I think we should start singing now". I said.

She hurriedly put lid on cakes, 'things' back in her bag and trotted off to her seat. She then trotted back to her bag on the table, got out her lyric folder, and did a second trot back to her seat.

"Sorry, I'd forget my head if it was loose" she said.

"Oh and me" chimed in Ann, you know I went to look for my reading glasses last night, and I had them on". They both chucked at the image.

"Right, that's lovely, but can we start now me dears" I continued....and so, breathing exercises commenced.

We were a couple of minutes in to this when Eileen arrived puffing and panting as she came through the door.

"Oh no, am I late, oww I've had a terrible time, I'm late 'aren't I?" she then began a full on group debate as to how much the parking fee for her car was, or should be.

"How long did you get Eileen"? I asked over the din.

"An hour" she replied.

"Oh you need longer than that love" I continued "were going to be here longer than an hour".

She decided be it right or wrong that instead of letting her hour be used up and going back out the car park to 'top it up' she would just get another ticket now. There was no talking her round she'd made up her mind. I have never heard such a who-har over "who's got 20p's and 50p pieces for the meter". By now it's 1.55pm, we haven't sang a note.......(not through want of trying) we'd only just managed to complete the breathing exercises.

20p's and 50p's were donated in various forms and then 'just' as I thought it would be a resolved issue as Eileen was on her way out, Maureen called,

"Oh there's some cake for you in that tupperwear Eileen", pointing towards the cake island, and yet another delay as she stopped, popped off the lid and lovingly glared over the pretty cakes. During this episode, Ian from the venue we were rehearsing in had kindly come in and replaced a chair with a wonky leg......the chair, Ian didn't have a wonky leg! (Always best to explain these things).

We then waited as broken chair was removed and several people 'had a go' at sitting in the 'new' chair. It wasn't a swivel chair, it wasn't Edwardian, or even state of the art. It was just.....a chair. So why all the excitement of so many trying it out for size I hear you cry (cry, being the operative word here)....because, it was blue! Yes, you read that correctly, blue. As opposed to the other seats which were pink. Don't even try to understand that, I tried, not worth it trust me. I decided we should start singing.

"Right everyone, page 7 'I Could Have Danced All Night'.
"Is this the one from Oliver"? Asked Doris.
"No, hee hee ya tray cloth" confirmed Maggie, "this is from My Fair Lady, oww it's a lovely show, I saw it once at the Theatre Royal, I don't think I have ever seen such a beautiful production, owww smashin' costumes. Your thinking of TOMORROW, TOMORROW, I LOVE YA, TOMORROW, Ohhh I remember once...."......and I stopped her in her tracks.
"Woe Maggie, let's just sing it shall we, and then in the break you can talk about it yeh. Oh by the way, 'Tomorrow' is from 'Annie', both shows though, Annie and Oliver are about orphans though so I see how you would mix it up"?
She mumbled something and turned her nose up like I'd just ripped up her winning lottery ticket. Oh dear. I tried again, "Right, I Could Have Danced All Night, here we go, and...."........'I could have danced all night, I could have danced all night and still have begged for mo'......... All of a sudden Madge says, "Oh look there's Ian" looking out of the window. Now why this would have been of interest when it was only five minutes previous he was standing right in front of us is anyone's guess. However, it seemed, 'I' was wrong, and it 'was' of interest.
Just on her way out of the door with a handful 'and' mouthful of cake, Eileen did a quick about turn "Ow, *munch munch* I wonder if he could *munch munch* do my wotsit parking ticket thingy while he's *munch munch* out there, save me legs".......and then she was gone!
I looked out of the window only to see Eileen chasing (chasing? well that 'run' that older ladies do, where the 'run' involves thrusting your elbows back and forth quite forcefully while your legs don't really go any faster than walking!) after a poor chap who indeed wasn't Ian. It was a man with a similar coloured shirt. Easy mistake, with Eileen, 'gone', I decided to start up the

singing again amidst the now chat about Ian, Eileen, change for the meter, 'Oliver', 'Annie' and Emmerdale! Yes, we'd gone onto yet another subject.

"Ok, Ok, I called out, please, ladies and gents, let's get these songs sung if we possibly can, we only have just under 2 hours now to rehearse". Order was restored.

"I could have danced all night, I could have danced all night and still have begged for more. I could have spread my wings and done a thou…….."

"OUCH, Ow Ow Ow". I suppose you'd say living up to the song I see Irene dancing around her chair.

"Irene what's wrong?" I ask.

"Cramp, cramp, ow ow, it just comes on when ya least expect it" she said "It must be that flamin' op I had in January, I get it regular now".

"I wish I did". Came a male voice from the back of the room, and teenage giggles went through the group like a dose of salts.

"Alright, alright" I said trying to get some kind of order.

She continued "I think I did a bit too much yesterday, I said to Iris next door, I'll pay for this gardening ya know".

"Is that Iris that used to be married to Geoff, lived in the bungalows round the back of Welbeck Street" asked Maggie

"Yes, that's her" said Irene, "why? Do you know her"?

"Know her! I had a right 'to do' with her over Geoff right in the middle of Morrisons. Accused me of allsorts when they were going through their split"

"Oww did she" continued Irene "Why? It wasn't you and him that were….."

"No, ow no" said Maggie "It was me sister, our Barbara, we look similar except I've got blonde hair and she's brunette, well we used to be, we don't speak anymore".

Irene turned and looked at Cath sitting at the other side of her,

"Um, you know Barbara, Cath" she said.

"It was her who won that holiday when you and your Mick had that flood in ya kitchen, we did let her know, but she didn't help did she (Irene knowing Barbara was at the time married to a plumber).......no........didn't help at all did they.......mind you, that aside she always kept a beautiful front step".

Thrilling as it was I felt the need to resume the lesson so, "Ladies, ladies, bless ya, right, come on now, look the time is creeping up to a quarter to three and we've hardly done anything".

There were mutterings around the room that followed agreeing with my statement and also, secretly asking who Iris and Geoff were!

We start the singing again............."...and still have begged for more. I could've spread my wings and done a thousand things, I've never done before"....."GOOD", I call "I'll never know what made it soooo, excitinggggg, why all at once my heart tooook flight. I on-ly know when he, began to dance with me I could've da...................."

And in mid-flight we were once again brought to an abrupt halt. I look over and on the back row hear another drama unfolding, "Is everything OK at the back there"? I call out.

"Oh, Oh noooooo". It was a collective chorus of no's actually.

"What's wrong now?" I ask.

"I'm so sorry, I must've forgotten to put the top on me bottle properly and the damned waters gone everywhere, I'm soaked" says Gill.

"You're soaked, you're soaked, what about my bag and coat, they're covered" shrieks Joan.

And just at the point where I thought things had calmed down the immediate three rows turned and scuffled to the back row with help and hindrance.

I stood and watched holding onto the top of my head.........

"Alright, er, listen ladies, go to the toilets or wherever you need to go and sort yourselves out, in the meantime the rest of you while the ladies are doing that lets at least sort out your lyrics so we have them in the correct order for this evening, then that will be one job we can get out of the way". I see lots of head nodding and positive gestures.

"So.....this is the number order you'll be doing the songs in OK, you all ready?, 3, 5, 7, 18........."

Janet "did she say 9, 7"?

Ann, "nooo FIVE, 7". Much faffing with lyric sheets followed.

Me "The next ones are 11, 9, 17"

"What was that 19"? Say's Doris.

Me "No, 9 and then 17"

"So what numbers are they again" says Bill..........

Me "3, 5, 7, 18"......I pause......."11, 9, 17"

"Right, is that it then"? Sheila asks.

"No, no" I say "that's just the first 7, you need to add 19, 13 and 4 to those and there is your first set"

"So how many sets are we doing"? Says John.

"Just the two" I say.

"Oh well this is all very well, I thought we'd be out of there for 8 o'clock" he grumbled.

"John, we'll be lucky if were out of 'here' for 8 o'clock at this rate" I say. "Look let's just do this as quickly as possible and then we can carry on with the singing".

At that point I notice the ladies of the bottle tipping drama have re-entered the room. And they're not on their own. They are swiftly followed by Eileen. Yes she's back. Ahh bless Eileen, the word 'lackadaisical' was invented for her!.................. ☺

"Phew, phew, phew" she puffed "Ow I'm right out of breath, eh it wasn't Ian ya know" she walked towards her chair, white curly hair bouncing along in time to her step......."but you'll never guess who it was"? She stopped, grabbed hold of her chin, head tilted in a 'thinker' kind of pose and followed on "Ow I forget his name now, but Ann, you know him, he used to work in Woolworths when your lad was there. Anyway I asked him if he remembered him".

"Awww and did he" Ann called back.

"No", said Eileen while dipping in her handbag and arriving at her chair.

"Eileen duckie, can we get you settled now, we've only done one song and sorted the lyrics so far, we are quite behind time" I said still optimistic.

"Yes my love, I'm all yours" she announced with hands up in surrender position, "now then, where did I put me readers' could've swore I put them in me bag this morning".

Ann sat there and smiled obviously remembering her previous chat about reading glasses and then..."Oh I said that earlier, couldn't find mine, had 'em on me head, hee hee hee".

'Were we still in Sunday'? I asked myself, I felt as if I'd been in that room all weekend.

I was now worrying..........It was 5 past 3, we had less than an hour to go through a further 19 songs. It wasn't going to happen was it!

I decide going through the songs in full couldn't happen if we were to get through the whole two sets. So I announced....

"I've had a thought everyone, starting with the first set we are just going to top and tail the songs, that way we should have a chance at looking at each of them, even if it's only briefly"

"Top and what"? Said Bernard.

"Top n tail", replies Maureen while scratching some past dinner from the front of her cardi.

"What does that mean?" "Never in all my years have I heard that one" asks Doreen looking over at me screwing her nose up.

"It just means we sing the first bit and last bit of the songs so that you can get to grips with the tempo we'll be singing them at and get a feel for them, we'll just be doing a few bars of the beginning and at the ends of each song", I look at them all and give a little smile as if confirming that 'was' going to happen. I could sense this hadn't been received well.

"Eh, I don't understand, well is that how were going to do them tonight, what's the point of learning a song if we're only going to do bits of 'em" asked a confused Doreen.

Maggie leaned forward like a shot "Ow don't be daft, we ARE doing the full songs tonight, didn't you hear what she just said", and then she 'tutted' in disgust.

I tried my best to defuse the conversation as 'top and tailing' became 'tap and tumbler', 'top and bottom', and my personal favourite 'tip and tamper'. Yes...everyone was now in full voice discussing what exactly 'top and tail' meant..........Emmerdale stood no chance.

"HELLO" I called out "HELLO, can we just get back to the songs....YES, we are singing the songs in full tonight Doreen, but just for now, let's just do them this way.........and......er........yeh........". Time was ticking by, it was then I seriously asked myself if I'd been hi-jacked by aliens as John waltzed over to the front of the class and rubbing his hands and doing three slow claps called for order as he just wanted to have a word about a fund raiser he was holding in October!!!!!

"No, no, NO JOHN", I said.........."no please, not now, please do that later, tonight, any time, but not now".

He casually strolled back to his seat with mutterings of October and how the bowling club had put a lot of work and time into it. I knew the feeling.

I tried again,

"Owww were not getting very far are we, right, let's do these as swiftly and easy as possible", all eyes were on me and I thought 'right, we can do this, yes we can do this'..........until I noticed Eileen bending her head down creeping out of the back of the class, obviously making herself invisible by her stance.

"Eileen, where you off to now" I asked.

"Er, me car, I'm just worried, I don't want to get into trouble, I've had such a lot on lately, my knees are playing up, I can't loose me licence. I'd be lost without it, I hate using buses and a've only just had it washed"............

The delicate sound of desert tumble weed as it blows in the wind wafted through my head as I try to understand the link. I can't.

........I decide even though there is only just under an hour to go before our time runs out, we should take a little break, let them talk out whatever they need to talk out, and try again with the last 30 minutes or so concentrating on the weaker songs. I announce this, "Ok everyone, coffee break and we'll start again in 15 minutes, if you just go through to the back room everything you need is in there, and there's some fresh milk in the fridge". Everyone is happy. Well, almost everyone.

May.... "I don't like coffee, is it just coffee? Is there any tea, I'd sooner have a cup of tea. Only I used to drink coffee at one time, that's all I would drink, coffee, coffee, coffee, then I just woke up one day not so'long back and realized it was 'that' that was giving me wind".

I walked out of the room, pushed open the fire door, closed it behind me and sat on the steps. Keep Calm Shelley, keep calm.....

This time tomorrow it will all be done and I'll be wondering why I got into such a state" I told myself.

Fifteen to twenty minutes later with refreshed oldies we started the songs. Eileen during the little coffee/tea/valium break had phoned Myra whom she sat next to in class to inform her that she was in the car park, sitting in her car. She'd decided (I was told) that she wouldn't be at the remainder of the lesson because she wanted to fill up her car with petrol, and didn't like doing it when the schools were coming out! She'd see us at the hotel later and what time did we have to be there for. I told Myra we would need to be there for 7.15pm at the very latest as we started at 7.30pm. The strange thing that baffled me then and now is the woman gets behind the wheel of a car'? Sobering thought isn't it!

The lesson continued and songs were resolved. "I think we should be alright" I convinced myself. Five minutes from the end of the lesson the lady from reception knocks on the door and says "Sorry to bother you, there's a lady on the phone, she wants to know the address of the hotel for this evening"?..........Eileen!!!!! Myra chimes in "Oh dear, shall I go and speak to her". "Yes please duckie if you would" I say "thank you", and as the group continue with the final song I can't help but worry, 'would we ever see Eileen again'!!!!

I have a confession to make. When everyone had left the room I also had a sit in the 'blue chair'! Well..............I wanted to know what all the fuss was about, and if it was actually (quote) "Owww a lot comfier than the pinks one's"........but no surprises really, it wasn't.

After the, er…. 'lesson'?, I rushed home had a quick shower, and put the glad rags on, back in the car and headed to the hotel. I arrived there for 6.30pm. This was a private function, a gentleman's 70th birthday, and I wanted it to go as smooth as possible. On arriving at the hotel his wife greeted me within seconds at the main doors.

"Oh hello, we are all really looking forwards to the singing" she said with a huge smile.

"Ohhh goooood" I said.

"We sat down at 6 for the meal" she explained "and they are just about to serve the main. Oh its lovely, Ron is having such a nice time, the hotel have done us proud as I know you and your choir will"

"Ohhhhhhhhh" I said…apprehensively. "Well as requested" I said "It's musicals all the way, I hope you and Ron like the choice of songs".

"Oh I'm sure we will" she beamed.

And with that the very neat smiley lady went back into the function room and left me sitting in the foyer where one by one and sometimes in twin-set twos, the singers arrived looking very nicely turned out indeed. I'd asked them to just wear any combination of black and white, and they had followed the instructions perfectly looking very smart and in some cases glamorous. Like teens they stood and chatted, giggled and were very excitable. It wasn't unlike an American prom night!

'Oh good, good, this is a good sign' I thought. After the afternoons 'non lesson' I was worried they would be a little subdued, but actually they were really quite upbeat. Well, not all of them, most of them were. I say that as we didn't have a full quota. I was waiting for 27 people and I had 24……We had no Janet, no Edie and………oh dear, no Eileen!

We waited and waited, it was now 7.29pm……..The lovely neat lady came out and assured us there was no rush, and it would be fine to start just after 8pm if we'd prefer…..Ron and his best pal of 63 years were doing little speeches, and gifts were being presented. So via hotel staff we sourced a room to leave coats, bags etc generally chill out before the event. I advised everyone to do some warming up exercises while I try and get hold of our missing ladies.

As I reached reception a taxi pulled up and out got Janet and Edie.

"Oh thank goodness" I said rushing towards them "Is everything OK, I was beginning to get worried".

Edie shook her head as Janet said "Well we've been at mine waiting for Eileen to pick us up, but she never turned up, is she here?"

It appears Eileen had promised both ladies a lift to and from the performance venue the previous week.

"Oh dear she must have forgotten ladies" I say "Never mind you're here now, I'll drop you off after if you like, but for now you see that door just there" (I said pointing) "that's where the others are. You can leave your coats and bags in there".

And off the pair trotted like two little girls.

It reached almost 8pm and I decide with the very neat and now patient lady we should start regardless. I'm instructing the group to come out of the room so that I can lock it and through the double doors of the reception in stumbles Eileen, in………..red!!!

Bright red, top to toe, red blouse, red skirt, red cardigan, red sparkly scarf, red shoes. Without a hint of a prompt George starts singing "Lady in Redddd".

"Er, George, no love, they can hear us through there" (gesturing towards to party room).

"Eileen, why are you in red"? I turned around and presented in a game show host fashion that everyone else was in black and white.

"Oh, oww, I knew there was something I'd meant to ask you this afternoon….Oh I'll be alright, should I stand at the end of the line?" she said.

"Yes" and I shook my head in disbelief and just decided to make the best of it all….Ok, so the show wasn't on time, and Eileen wasn't in black and white, just blips, we'll be fine…………….fine.

So in we go to the party headquarters.

The room cheer!.............I was surprised…….so were the singers….and they instantly grinned from ear to ear like rock stars entering an arena.

Without any squabbles or dithering they all lined up nicely ready for the off.

"Yes" I thought "I think everything will be ok".

We began the show……………………

"The best of times is now, what's left of summer but a faded rose……..the best of times is now, as for tomorrow well who knows, who knows who knows…………….etc.

We finished……….audience clapped appreciatively.

It appeared to all be going well.

Time passed and we're now nine songs in, smiling faces around the room, smiling faces within the choir……….me, even I had a smiley face, and then as I was announcing our last song of the first set…………………..

WHOOSH…………..like an origami style wedding day, Eileen's lyric sheets had slipped out of her folder while she was scratching her head and they flew left, right and centre, and were scattered all over the floor in front of us. The audience laughed. I accepted that, it was unexpected, and things going wrong. Well

I guess when you're in the audience it's all part of the fun isn't it, plus something to tell the neighbours when you get home…..like.

"Oh that Lesley Garrett, she's a card isn't she……there she was walking out onto the stage at the Royal Albert Hall, and the heal breaks on her shoe and she goes flying, how we laughed"……..that sort of thing!!! The fact she is a stunning opera singer in one of the world's finest venues would be immaterial. I'm sure that has never happened to Ms. Garret, and I hope it never does, but had it, I'm sure it would be one of the major talking points for the audience members the following day.

Meanwhile…….myself, Maggie, Janet and even the birthday boy Ron, are all on our hands and knees picking up lyric sheets, while Eileen stands there with her hands on her hips saying,
"Well, I don't know how that's happened"!!!!…………….Oh, give me strength.
"Eileen" I call…….."EILEEN".
She glances over to me with not a care in the world.
 "What"?
"Can you help us pick these up please"? I say.
"Ow no I can't bend with my legs" she says, as she turns and asks the woman on the near table if she could have a drink of water……Oh for the love of……………..
The audience, carry on laughing. Eventually the lyric sheets are collected and ladies go back to their positions. I thank the birthday boy and encourage his guests to give him a round of applause. While this is happening, I gesture to Maggie who is standing close by to Eileen to help get her lyrics sorted out for the last song of the set.
I then do a little comedy routine to help with the confusion and try and save the first set. It gives the ladies time to sort out

the lyrics and the rest of the gang to re-group. Well, that was the plan.

This next paragraph comes with some sound advice.

'Never try to do comedy surrounded by a group of amateurs'. They just don't 'get it' when your being ironic, ad-libbing, or .... doing comedy! I was being heckled from every direction....by MY singers! However, I must have learned something in my trade as I managed to hold it together, and make it entertaining for the audience, as well as the choir. At that point I seriously tried to channel Doris Stokes as I certainly didn't appear to be getting through to anyone else!

With the first set finished we scuttled back to our little room and safe haven where drinks and nibbles had lovingly been left for us. I kept a distance. Even though the singing was going really well, it's easy to lose your grip on the reins if you give out too much praise too soon, so I hovered near the reception sipping on a little glass of orange juice.

The fifteen minutes of break time were up and as the clock now headed towards 9.20pm (we were running so late) I once again gathered the gang together and back into the room we went. No sooner had we reached our starting block, off we went........

"I could have danced all night, I could have danced all night, and still have begged for more.............I could have spread my wings and done a........."......etc. I stood there waving my arms about conducting as if I'm bringing in a Boeing 707, when I suddenly realize, we have no Eileen. What was wrong with me! How had I missed this, she was dressed from head to toe in bright red. I continue, and we eventually finish the song. Ron and wife stand up, with arms raised and clapping over their heads in appreciation, their guests applaud too. It appeared that song was very special to them. It was just by chance I included it. Just as

I turn and acknowledge the kind applause I notice Eileen at the back of the room, drinking tea from a cup and saucer, chatting to a random lady.

Now! KILL ME NOW!

She is totally unaware she should be up at the front with the choir singing it would seem. So I announce the next song........"Ladies and Gentlemen, we hope you'll enjoy this next song, from 'High Society' this is "Who Wants To Be A Millionaire"...I decide to tag on the end "Eileen, come on love"...the group pick up on this in an instant and we get a half full rendition of "Come On Eileen".

I smile trying to convince myself 'it'll be ok'!

She then makes her way through the tables, introducing herself like the Queen Mother on a royal visit at every stop. She reaches the performing area, the group cheer, the audience cheer. The lady in red, adjusts her necklace, hair, lyric folder and then looks at me as though she's been standing there waiting for us to start for the past ten minutes.

The second song begins and wow, the singers are really giving it their all, it sounds great (do I sound shocked.......well, actually I was!). Half way through this song, I split it so that there are a few solo's within the group. Eileen take's this opportunity half way through the song, YES, half way through the song to explain to Maggie why she was at the back of the room....and insisting on being louder than the soloists......The room starts to titter.

"You see I didn't realize you'd started" she said "Only I want my living room curtains to be in that colour. The colour of that ladies skirt, and I asked her where she got it from 'cos I thought well if it's cheap I can go and get one and take it to B&Q for the man to mix up the colour for me"...

I stood there conducting thinking, 'should I bother to carry on'.......'I wonder what time it is now' and 'it was this time last week I was in Germany singing at a really high class event........and now I'm doing this, umm interesting'.

She continues, "At first I thought that lady was our Debra, do you know our Debra"? She asks a wilting Maggie, and by wilting I mean trying to look as invisible as possible.

"No" says Maggie in a dipped head and hushed voice.

"Oh ya do" insists Eileen, she used to go out with, ow what's his name, that lad who played your son when we did Mame".

Maggie is now interested............well...................there was nothing else of importance happening was there. ☹

"Do you mean lovely Daniel" says Maggie, still in a hushed tone.

"Tut, yes, that's him, what a lovely lad. Well ya know when he left the area for that job, they split up. I knew it wouldn't last with him being in London, well Ipswich, so it wa' as good as. Our Debra really let herself go, didn't go out, didn't do anything, just ate, oww she was a big gell.......She's alright now though, her Mam, our Jackie, told me she's had one of them brass bands fitted so she's lost a load've weight"...

Maybe it's me.............maybe I expect too much.

Are you possibly sitting there thinking "why on earth would she write all this down"............Well I can answer that easily.

A, I couldn't believe it was happening at the time, and

B, In the back of my mind, I thought 'maybe one day when this is a distant memory and I no longer need therapy, I'll write all this down in a book'.

We get through the next few songs with ease and then we come to the last one. I'm just about to say a few words to the party people when Eileen says as loud as you like,

"Oh Janet, I should've picked you up shouldn't I"?
The audience, bless them, at this point are in raptures. Janet nods with pursed lips and Edie on the front row is nodding in agreement.
Eileen had one of those 'Mrs Slocombe' accents (Re T.V comedy 'Are You Being Served') not quite posh, but not quite common, and it just sounded hysterical.
"Oww sorry" Eileen carries on, "I was on my way out of the door and then I realized I hadn't taken my pills or programmed the recorder thingy for Eastenders".
You missed out there Emmerdale!
I glance around at the audience who have either had far too much to drink, or are on medication themselves as they laugh hysterically at the red lady.
We eventually limp to the final song. 'That's Entertainment'... that's not me making a statement, that was the song title.
It is performed while big smiles gleam towards us from every corner of the room...........all but Janet and Edie that is who are, £8 down...But the crowd are clapping along and generally having a fine old time.
We reach the finishing line...................YES...........we did it, we got there. It may be 10.25pm, we may have had some mishaps, but we did it, we finished.
People release party poppers, and cheers go up, for us, for the birthday boy, for mankind in general.............Wa'hey.

I go to the bar to get a large glass of lime and soda whilst the choir flutter about like excited butterflies back and forth around each other to congratulate themselves.
"Well done everyone" I call as I make my way towards the back of the room "well done". I make my way from the bar, drink in

hand, neat wife and Ron walk towards me..........."Oh dear" are my first thoughts.

"Shelley" he says..........."that was.............oh.............that was........"

I wait for the next bit of his sentence thinking to myself how many ways and languages is it possible to say sorry in?

"That was........fantastic" he says............eh? It was fantastic?

"I have never laughed so much in ages, have we love" he said with his arm around his little neat wife.

"No" she joined in all very smile-y ☺ "Oh the comedy aspect of the choir is so funny, we loved it. Our friends are all saying how funny you are at keeping such a serious face at times, it made it all the funnier......how long have you been teaching them, I love the comedy twist you've put on everything"

I'm astonished......in shock I say..."Three months. I've been teaching them twice a week for the past three months".

"No? Really! Well.... we've loved every minute of it, ha ha ha, Oh we'll be laughing about this tomorrow wont we Ron" said the tiny neat wife. Ron then gave me a mighty firm 'gents' handshake (ouch) and strolled off to collect all his gifts and cards he'd been presented with that evening.

'Well, well, well, I didn't see that coming', I thought, and admittedly I was in slight shock. With the drink, drank, I went to find Edie and Janet. Back in the reception area I could see a sea of black and while with this flash of red in the middle, 'Oh now what', were my thoughts.

It's Eileen............of course it is..........she is in desperate need to give Julia her 50p back, previously given to her during the afternoon. It causes more confusion than the opening of parliament. I hear Bernard say quite reasonably,

"Oh Eileen, she's already gone, leave it until you see her again, I don't think on this occasion she'd mind. Not like you're going to leave the country is it"? He said sarcastically.

"I KNOW" says Eileen, quite loudly for some unknown reason..."But the funny thing is I just went to my car 'cos I thought I'd need to get the man out 'cos me lights keep staying on, and in the glove compartment, I find this little purse. Forgot all about it hadn't I and it's full of 50's, 20's and ten's, there's about £7 in it, ya know as an emergency for car parks n' that". (Me – *bangs head against wall*). She then made a bee-line for me..........

"Oh I need to get going Eileen" I say, trying to make a hasty exit.

"Yes I know but I just need to tell you this" (I thought 'hang on a moment I think there might be an apology in the offering here').

"It wasn't my fault" she says.

"What? Eh? What wasn't your fault?" I stupidly ask.

Eileen carries on "The real reason I was late, well, yes I was late and it was my fault, but it wasn't if you see what I mean. I'd forgotten to take my tablets and I need to tape 'Corrie', it threw me 'cos it's not normally shown on a Sunday is it? Why do they do that? Keep flippin' swappin' n changing programmes round, drives me mad, anyway, the tape was nearly at the end so I had to use me 'Summer Wine' tape, but I've been proper upset all damned day".

"Because of the car parking?" I ask sympathetically.

"NO..........ya daft appeth" she says "Because of that Shirley at the Parkside Players (amateur dramatic society). I didn't take those costumes. I borrowed one hat, one hat. Well I say one hat, I kept a shawl, and a gold bow tie, oh oh and an Alice band that had a robin on it, but that was all, that's not stealing is it"? She said running her fingers through her hair.

"Not if you say so, now I really must go" I say, now gradually moving backwards in a strange attempt to get closer to the main doors.

She starts again "You see if I'd have taken a costume, I'd have said 'I've taken a costume', but just a bit of ribbon, lace n that, it doesn't count does it, and I'll tell you something else................"
I've now walked so far backwards towards the door people were thinking I'd just arrived.
"Arrrhhhhh look" I say (almost crying!) there's John, "JOHN" I call out as if I hadn't seen him in a year....."There you go Eileen, tell John all about yer, er, er, bye, bye..........byyyeeeeee".
And with that I got the attention of my two passengers and escaped out of the main entrance, we then legged it to the car. On getting inside my little car all three of us sighed with relief. Despite the chatter, it all seemed very tranquil and quiet after such a confusing, hectic evening. Dropping off the ladies and then arriving home I quickly changed into comfy clothes and made a coffee. Hello caffeine, oh how I've missed you!

The day should have started at 1pm and gone through until 9pm with a little break to nip home and get changed........My day started at 12.30 and I eventually arrived home at 11.15pm. However I was back in the comfort of home, feet up, coffee in hand and a nice film about to start on the TV. Just as the credits of the film started to roll, *ping* went my phone. It was a text message from Evelyn (who you know as the small neat lady) it read........

"Shelley, thank you so much for tonight. Everyone had a lovely time. Ron is delighted. Thank you. Thought you should know one of your singers left their cardi......................."

Guess what colour it was?!!!...........................*turns TV volume up, closes eyes*.

Makes the 'frog' episode look relatively easy!!!!

Do you know an 'Eileen'? If so, I believe there is a help line!

Favourite overheard quote of the time.

"........I didn't realize I'd fallen down the last few stairs knocking that man at the side of me, everything just went black, I knew I was laying down 'n' I thought I'd died an' then I looked down at me feet and all I could see was a bald head and a trilby hat at the side of it. So I just lay there.......Have you been to that theatre? Owww the ceiling is really beautiful."

..............right then, I'm off to sew a button on my hat!

CHAPTER TITLES – SONG REFERENCES

I SAW HER STANDING THERE – THE BEATLES (Lennon/McCartney) 1963

OH I DO LIKE TO BE BESIDE THE SEASIDE – British Music Hall
(John A. Glover-Kind) 1907

YOU CAN LEAVE YOUR HAT ON – Various Artistes (R. Newman) 1972

HELLO – LIONEL RICHIE (L. Richie) 1984

TALK TO YOUR DAUGHTER – ROBBEN FORD (J.B. Lenoir) released 1988

LOVE ME LOVE MY DOG – PETER SHELLEY (P. Shelley) 1975

RIGHT SAID FRED – BERNARD CRIBBINS (T. Dicks/M. Rudge) 1962

RUN RABBIT RUN – FLANAGAN AND ALLEN (N. Gay/R. Butler) 1939

I THINK I LOVE YOU – THE PARTRIDGE FAMILY (T. Romeo) 1970

TAKE ME I'M YOURS – SQUEEZE (C. Difford/G. Tilbrook) 1978

FOOD GLORIOUS FOOD – Musical 'OLIVER' (L. Bart) 1960's

PAPA CAN YOU HEAR ME – Musical 'YENTL' - BARBRA STRIESAND
(M. Legrand/A. Bergman/M. Bergman) 1983

IT'S A GRAND NIGHT FOR SINGING – Musical 'STATE FAIR'
(Rogers/Hammerstein) 1945

(SPOOKY – Various Artistes (Shapiro/H. Middlebrooks Jr) 1967

STRANGE MAGIC – ELO (Electric Light Orchestra) 1975

LADY IN RED – CHRIS DE BURGH (C. De Burgh) 1986